Praise for

Semi-Colon
A Writer's Cheeky Journey
Through Colorectal Cancer

"Neil has shown us all that humour is a wonderful way to cope with a disease that is not always so funny. He made us all "crack a smile" for years at our annual comedy fest and encouraged patients across the country with his infectious personality. His easy manner, compassion and devotion to the cause have not only made thousands of Canadians aware of colon cancer, but he has inspired and provided hope to so many of us. Neil has documented his journey in a way that is not only entertaining, but demonstrates his unique insight to life's challenges."

- Barry Stein
President, Colorectal Cancer Association of Canada

Semi-Colon

A Writer's Cheeky Journey
Through Colorectal Cancer

by Neil Crone

echo
BOOKS

An imprint of
Wintertickle PRESS

Semi-Colon

A Writer's Cheeky Journey
Through Colorectal Cancer

Cover Photo: Rob Johnson
Cover and Book Design: Heather Down
Copy Editing: Patricia MacDonald

ISBN 978-1-894813-74-7

Published by Echo Books, an imprint of Wintertickle Press
Suite 155
132 Commerce Park Drive, Unit K
Barrie, ON, Canada   L4N 0Z7

WintertticklePress.com
facebook.com/WintertticklePress

ĕß

echo
BOOKS

An imprint of

Wintertickle **PRESS**

To all my friends in the chemo chair
and to all those holding their hands.
With special love to Suzanne, Duncan and
Connor…thanks for pulling me through.

Acknowledgements

The cover photo was graciously taken by Rob Johnson. For more information or inquiries about Rob Johnson's photography, please contact him via email at bobstate@me.com.

Thanks also goes out to surgeon Martin Stewart for the loan of all medical supplies and to Francine Reid for her dad's old typewriter. What a gem.

Gratitude is extended to copy editor Patricia MacDonald for her patience and extended work on this project.

This is a collection of columns and emails. The columns were originally published in select Metroland newspapers. Both content and style have been edited from the original to better suit the format of the book.

Much of this book is opinion and should not be taken as medical advice. Although Wintertickle Press is committed to publishing works of quality and integrity, the opinions expressed are the author's alone and not necessarily those of Wintertickle Press.

Please realize that this collection of writing is for entertainment purposes only. If you have medical concerns or questions, please seek qualified medical advice.

Contents

Foreword

There is nothing even remotely funny about cancer. However, this eclectic collection of musings somehow brings smiles and hope to an often grim topic. Through his personal experiences, Neil manages to transport the reader through the nuances of a strange, very difficult—but somehow beautiful—journey.

This isn't a book *just* for people affected by the disease. The insights and life observations transcend the circumstance of cancer and can easily be translated into the wilful act of living life out loud.

The newspaper articles span many years, beginning even before Neil was diagnosed with cancer. Although all very different, the columns are tied together by a common thread of thoughtfulness, unique observation and yes, cancer.

This book is a collection, and as a collection it portrays snippets of a life, not necessarily a linear, cleanly ordered chronicle. Instead, it is untidy, similar to the messiness of living.

Even though the columns and emails jump around, they manage to cling together nicely through theme and thought. Arranged as such, it makes it easy for this book to be read cover to cover or simply picked up and quotes, columns and emails read at random.

Wishing all readers peace, hope, love and health.

"Cancer is a word,

not a sentence."

– John Diamond

Introduction

Somewhere in the vicinity of the millennium—I can never exactly be sure of when it started because, being a male, I am endowed with the superhuman ability to ignore any and all signs of illness until the very last minute—I began to notice I was having what I will refer to as "bum" issues. And just so we understand one another, I was not undergoing an infestation of homeless persons or transients, I was experiencing a little bleeding from the tuchus, the heinie—my *butt*. Nothing huge or too startling, mind you, just a little streaking on the occasional stool and now and again a little on the old TP.

Again, for the longest time, being a man, I was able to find any number of ways to ignore the warning signs my body was eagerly waving at me:

"So, it's a little blood…who the hell doesn't bleed from their butt now and again?"

"Probably just something I ate."

"There, see? It's gone. Haven't had it for weeks."

In retrospect, I know, of course, that the logical thing, the smart thing, the healthy—even self-loving—thing to do would've been to go see a doctor. Not a big deal. Really. I had a doctor at the time. A very good doctor. And his office was literally only a block or two from my home. But did I go to see him? No. Of course not. Apparently I had much more important things to do. I had to mow the lawn, and screw things in and hammer stuff—you know, man stuff.

I don't understand why men are like this—why we have this aversion to taking the tiniest amount of time out to seek the advice of a medical professional when something seems amiss with our bodies. It must have some bizarre anthropological root. Somewhere in our DNA is the memory of that first unfortunate caveman who left his family for a few minutes to have a buddy pull a thorn out of his foot. When he returned, he discovered a sabre-toothed tiger had eaten his entire clan. Something like that.

At any rate, I put things off and put things off until, finally, my wife insisted that I make an appointment. This would be a fitting time, I think, to acknowledge the women in our lives. The plain fact of the matter is that were it not for the presence of women in the world and their insistence that we look after ourselves and seek help when help is needed, men, as a species, would've died off millennia ago. Men do many things very well (see aforementioned list of mowing, hammering and screwing…with a screwdriver), but when it comes to our health, it is nice to have a female around to put a much-needed governor on our stupidity. And trust me, she may tell you she is bothering you to see a doctor because she loves you—the other plain fact of the matter is that she is really doing it to get you to shut the hell up and quit complaining about your malady. And who could blame her?

And so, weeks, months or probably years after first exhibiting symptoms (again, who can tell when you're busy being a man), I finally found myself in a doctor's office. After a cursory examination, my GP told me it was more than likely a case of hemorrhoids. Not a big deal and fairly common among men my age, early 40s. Also quite treatable. He then set me up with an appointment to see a proctologist, a.k.a. bum doctor.

Now, if you think getting a man to go see a doctor is difficult, getting one to go and see a *bum* doctor is well nigh impossible. You may as well ask a man to stop screwing…with a screwdriver. Balk as I might, though, my wife was now fully ahead of the curve, and she let me know in no uncertain terms that any discomfort I might experience at the hands (and fingers) of said bum doctor would be nothing compared to what would most certainly befall me at home if I did not follow through with this. Again, God bless women.

Now, I'll be honest, I didn't like this bum doctor. His office was kind of grungy, and we didn't really hit it off. Not that I was expecting flowers and chocolates, mind you, but I like to at least get a vibe that my malady and I are more than just a medical insurance number to be processed. And sometimes you have to trust your gut—or your bum. He did the requisite peek up where the sun never shines and informed me that there was, in fact, a hemorrhoid that might be bleeding a little. He told me he could fix me up by banding it, a somewhat medieval process where the offending hemmie essentially has the life throttled out of it by a tight rubber band. He said it was a painless procedure and my issues would be over within a week or so. I should've noticed that his pants were on fire at that point in time, as he was clearly a big fat liar. In my defence, I was bending over and facing away from him, so I couldn't get a good look. When he snapped that sucker on, I almost went through the roof. It felt like he'd set a mousetrap off in my butt.

But I digress. Something else happened, or actually *didn't* happen, at that first meeting with the bum doctor that was probably more important than anything else. At one point during the examination he asked me if I'd ever been scoped. In other words, had I ever had a colonoscopy? I told him "no" and he kind of shrugged and said that, at 42, I was still pretty young for needing a scope. So, he didn't scope me.

In retrospect I wish he had. I *so* wish he had. And I wouldn't even have needed any anesthetic. That band thing was hurting so much he could've stuck a periscope up there, and I wouldn't have felt a thing. More to the point, had he insisted on taking a more detailed look, he would've no doubt discovered a small lesion on my colon just in the vicinity where it turned south and became my rectum. He may have caught my cancer before it had the chance to grow and spread to the point where I would require months of chemotherapy and radiation treatments. Maybe. Who really knows?

Do I blame him? No. Not really. I suppose he thought he was making a logical decision based on my age. I wish I had been more informed and able to take more responsibility for my own health. I wish I had known that there was a history of colon cancer in my family—that it had killed my grandfather and my aunt. I wish that my family had talked a little more about this stuff. Given that knowledge, I could have—and most certainly would have—requested a scope. You can bet your ass on that. Of course, I wasn't thinking about cancer or any of that stuff then. The only thing I was really aware of at that point in time was the jumper cable attached to the hemorrhoid in my behind. And so I hobbled to my car and drove home, thinking that that was the end of it.

But of course it wasn't. It was really just the beginning.

Almost two years later, still experiencing some bleeding, I went to see my GP again. I thought he might chastise me or at the very least laugh at me for once again not addressing my health issues until the eleventh hour. But he didn't. Even though he was a doctor, he was a man too, after all, and no doubt played the same Russian roulette with his own body. He wanted to send me back to Dr. Bad Vibe, but this time I spoke up. I asked him if he had any other options. He did. Enter Dr. Thoroughly Good. Within minutes of meeting with Dr. TG, he had insisted on and scheduled me for a full colonoscopy. More importantly, although neither of us knew it at that point, he had also just saved my life.

This collection of writing came about for a number of reasons—first and foremost to give hope, health and power to anyone with a cancer diagnosis and also to put things back into perspective. We are the ones with the power, not the cancer. Cancer is not always a death sentence. Cancer is not the bogeyman. It doesn't have to be the big C. It is simply a disorder—a misalignment of sorts. I want desperately to make people aware of their enormous, awesome and largely untapped potential to heal themselves and to experience peace in the process. I want to help caregivers and the families of cancer patients to find their ways through—and out of—the disease with as little stress and fright as possible.

And I want everyone, especially men, to get their heads around how easy, important and above all, normal it is to get a colonoscopy. This simple, non-invasive process could very well save your life.

Having said that last bit, believe me, I know where you're coming from, guys. I wasn't exactly looking forward to my first scope. I felt uncomfortable with the idea of taking a delivery where I'd previously made only shipments. And of course, like any unknown or first-time experience, the very word *colonoscopy* was shrouded in myth and urban legend. One of the worst things humans can ever do when faced with a new medical procedure is talk to another human about it. It seems, for a ridiculously large number of people, that it is never enough to simply listen to another person's fears and concerns about some imminent ordeal—they have to one-up them.

"I'd think twice about that, boy. I heard about a guy had his eye poked out from the inside when the doctor pushed too much hose in."

"Whatever you do, make sure they put you out. You wake up in the middle of that, you'd wished you'd died on the table!"

"Whatever you do, don't let 'em put you out! I knew a guy—never woke up. Died on the table!"

Don't listen to these people. And don't have them for friends. I've been scoped many times, and I can tell you it's completely painless. They put you into a nice deep sleep; a little while later you wake up, you fart like a vegetarian lumberjack—and you're good to go. True, the prep on the night before is not exactly fun, but it's not at all painful or anything to be afraid of. Just get yourself a pack of wet wipes and some decent bathroom reading material and you're all set.

Dr. TG scoped me and discovered what Dr. Bad Vibe might've caught two years earlier. The source of my bleeding was a lesion on my colon. And, because I'd been a dope and let it slide for two years, it was now too big to fix by going in through the back door, so to speak. Dr. TG told me he would have to perform abdominal surgery in order to repair the damage. Another step in the ridiculous ladder of things I might've saved myself from had I only listened to my body when it first spoke to me.

It's important to note at this point that I still didn't know that I had cancer. While Dr. TG was scoping me, he performed a biopsy of the lesion and the result came back negative. As far as he and I and everybody else were concerned, my surgery was simply to go in and solder the leak in my plumbing back together again. Still, simple or not, abdominal surgery is abdominal surgery, and I had been told to prepare myself for a fairly uncomfortable journey back to normal.

What I could not prepare myself for and what, again, was the furthest thing from my mind was awakening from the anesthetic to the news that upon opening me up, Dr. TG had discovered a peach-sized cancerous stage III tumour on the outside of my colon eating its hungry way through to the inside. I had *cancer*.

And that's where I'll leave you for now, because that's really where the emails, journal entries, columns and ponderings in the rest of this book began. They began as broadcast emails to friends and family at a time when I just didn't have the strength to answer all of their wonderful letters individually. And then, magically, they morphed into something more than that as I began to understand and appreciate the unspeakably rare gift that cancer had given me. They are the story of a person and the people he loves finding their way through the dark, frightening shadows of cancer, chemotherapy and radiation by following the unquenchable light of love, laughter, friendship and family. They are a testament to the remarkable power of connection and communication and saying yes to every single blessing offered you. I hope you may find something here that helps you as much as it helped me. I wish you happiness, health and every good thing. Because that's usually the order in which they show up. Blessings.

Subject: Chemo Is Like Being Pregnant

To: Group

From: Neil Crone

Priority: High

I'm starting to believe that being on chemotherapy is a lot like being pregnant. In my case, I get chemo every day for five days in a row. Then I get three weeks off to rest and let the body rebuild itself. The whole cycle takes about 30 days. Like a pregnancy, I can actually break my treatment down into trimesters. And the similarities are startling.

At the outset I am bubbling with enthusiasm, eager to read every book and Internet article I can get my hands on regarding the wonderful process going on in my body. I eat all the right things, exercise diligently and take good care of myself. I can't wait to hear the pitter-patter of little toxic feet. Not having been through this before, I am, of course, a little nervous too. Will it hurt? Don't be silly, I tell myself. Why, killing cancer cells is the most natural thing in the world. People have been doing it since the world began, you ninny.

In my second trimester, things aren't quite as rosy. The wonderful process begun in my first weeks has now become, quite frankly, a royal pain in the ass. I don't like my body so much anymore. I think I look awful. I feel nauseous a lot, and I rarely get off of the couch. I'm bitchy. I wear pyjamas all the time, my version of maternity wear.

Feeding me becomes an arduous guessing game. I may say I feel like eating one thing, and then the minute I sit down to a plate of it, the smell makes me gag. I am plagued by cravings, usually for things that are not at all good for me. After one chemo session I make my wife pull over so I can get a huge plateful of steak and eggs and home fries. Nothing on the plate is even remotely green. I inhale it, my wife staring in shock and smiling weakly. She knows better than to object. Believe me, you don't really want to get into it with a man in his second trimester of chemo.

By the time the third trimester rolls around, chemo patients—like their pregnant female counterparts—are fairly glowing. This is, however, nothing to do with hormones or the bliss of a prospective newborn. It's just the radiation treatments. Once you've been blasted with enough X-rays, you can read without a light on.

Finally delivery day arrives, and my IV tube is pulled out of me kicking and screaming. My jubilant wife and I beam with pride. They let me hold it for a while before taking it away. The weeks go by, and soon I am feeling better—more myself. After a while, remarkably, the pain and suffering of the first delivery are forgotten. And then as time passes, I find myself yearning for a second treatment. After all, I'm over 40 now, and there is some urgency. My biological clock is ticking away loudly.

So before we know it, we're happily doing it all over again, blissfully unaware of what's coming—the discomfort, the nausea, the cravings, the paralyzing fatigue. Why do we do it? For the same reason people get pregnant I guess. We're in love.

In gratitude,

Neil

"Once you choose hope,
anything's possible."

– Christopher Reeve

"Feed your faith,
and your fears will starve to
death."

– Anonymous

Victory over cancer best type of party

My eight-year-old came home the other day, flushed with excitement. His class was going to have a party the next day. It was going to be a big deal. I mentally ran through all the usual suspects; it wasn't Halloween, Christmas was long gone, Valentine's too, and it wasn't Easter yet. What was left? He then explained to me the whole class was celebrating the fact that one of the little girls in the class had just had her last chemotherapy treatment after a long and exhausting battle with leukemia. She was free and clear.

He skipped off happily, leaving me completely blown away. I loved him intensely for his naked enthusiasm about this party and his simple, childlike understanding of the reason for it, and I loved his teacher for having it. The fact was not lost on me for a second that, had that little girl and her cancer been in my Grade 3 class, there would more than likely have been no party. Tragically, there would have been nothing to celebrate—just an empty desk.

When I was in Grade 3, leukemia and chemotherapy were not part of our lexicon. I don't remember if any of the kids in my class had cancer or any other life-threatening illnesses. I probably wouldn't have known if they had. I remember Timmy P. seemed to have a perpetually snotty nose, and I'm pretty sure Wayne M. was a little "tetched in the head," but that was as far as it went.

People didn't talk about such things back then, certainly not in front of the children. It wasn't considered healthy. But here, now, in this little girl's class, the other kids had been aware of the illness from the get-go. And, more importantly, they'd been a big part of the healing process too. I remember two years ago, when this same little girl was first diagnosed, going to the school to videotape her classmates so that she, in the hospital, could remain connected to them and her old life somehow.

I remember crowds of pudgy, grinning faces in my viewfinder waving and screaming out their jubilant "get wells." I remember the walls of those classrooms plastered with pictures of this little girl in her hospital room, her smiling, freckled face beaming out from under a goofy hat that covered her newly bald head. I remember a community coming together to create a fund to help the little girl's family deal with new and crushing medical expenses, in stark contrast to the silent ignorance of my own Grade 3 world where no one knew. Now, we all knew, and I am convinced we were all better for it. The unexpected joy I felt upon hearing the reason for the little girl's party is proof enough of that statement.

I've thought about it for a while now, and I kind of wish the whole town had been invited to that classroom party. I would've gone. It's important that we share the grief in this life, but it's just as important, I think, that we share the cake.

Subject: Chemo Wedding Anniversary

To: Group
From: Neil Crone
Priority: High

My wife and I just celebrated our 18th wedding anniversary. We spent the day lavishly treating ourselves to a visit to the oncology ward in Oshawa for chemo cocktails and later a romantic interlude at Sunnybrook's radiation department. You may not think there's anything sexy about having two female lab technicians hauling your drawers down and X-raying your patootie, but some people pay big bucks for that kind of stuff. Here I was getting it for free. I didn't even have to fly to Thailand. The evening was capped off perfectly by a gourmet dinner for four (kids in tow) of burgers and fries. Does it really get any better than that?

As Suzanne and I lay in bed that night, accompanied by the mechanical whirring of my newly attached chemo pump, which lay between us like some kind of high-tech chastity belt, I asked her if, 18 years ago, she'd ever thought we'd be spending our anniversary like this. She laughed, mumbled an exhausted something or other, patted my pump and drifted off to a much-deserved sleep. But as I lay there, thinking in the dark, the past 14 hours or so playing themselves over in my head, it occurred to me just how nice a day it had been and how truly lucky we were to have one another. We had spent the day, as we spend most of our days these days, talking and laughing and listening to one another. Sharing each other's thoughts on everything from bowel movements to crossword puzzles (what's a four-letter word for chemotherapy—it starts with "F"). I also thought about how much we touch each other during a day. A hand squeeze, a light rub on the back in passing, fingers through my hair (what's left of it), a bare foot on top of a bare foot under the breakfast table. There are a million ways to tell someone you love them, from a passionate kiss to the changing of a dressing or the draping of a warm blanket over cold feet. And finally, I thought of our children, the real fruit of those 18 years. I thought about their patience and good humour throughout every one of these strange days and their simple, unbridled joy over nothing more than burgers and fries in the car. They are wonderful, fine little people that I cannot ever spend too much time with.

Finally, I thought about how all these pieces fit together so perfectly into the puzzle of my life. The puzzle that day by day, piece by piece, shows me more of why I am here and what it is I am supposed to be doing. Eighteen years ago I found that puzzle almost indecipherably difficult.

And so, with my beautiful friend and partner snoozing beside me, my chemo pump buzzing along like some tiny, malevolent sidekick and my boys deeply dreaming down the hall, I found I was able to answer my own question. No. There is no way in heaven I could ever have foreseen being so blissfully happy 18 years ago.

Love to all,

Neil

"Scars are tattoos
with better stories."

– Anonymous

"Tell your story by highlighting the victories. Because it's your victories that will inspire, motivate, encourage other people to live their stories in grander ways."

– Iyanla Vanzant

I was under the knife one year ago

It's difficult to believe, but exactly one year ago today, I was lying on an operating table with a pair of strange hands poking around inside me. An hour or so later, I gave birth to a bouncing baby tumour. It's a momentous anniversary to be sure, worthy of celebration. I'm just not sure how one goes about that.

What exactly is the one-year tumour anniversary? Paper? Saline? Plasma?

And more importantly, what exactly should I do to celebrate it? As the Wicked Witch of the West was so fond of saying, "These things need to be handled delicately."

My first thought is that it should be a very personal time between my surgeon and me. I mean, I don't know how much more intimate you can get with a person than actually having your hands inside them. Do you think handling somebody's colon counts as getting to first base? Again, I'm unsure. This is new territory.

Anyway, I picture the two of us having a romantic dinner in the hospital cafeteria, the place where we first met, staring happily into one another's eyes as I order for the two of us. "I'll have the stewed prunes and the doctor will have the gelatin… and a bottle of your best flat ginger ale as well."

I wonder how my wife will take it when I tell her, "Sorry honey, those flowers are for Dr. S."

Seriously, though, it does feel like something should be done. I'm alive thanks to that surgery. We go to a lot of trouble and expense to celebrate other events not nearly so worthy. Grey Cup parties, Halloween parties, Pancake Tuesday. Pretty diluted fare.

How come we don't hear about kidney transplant parties, Bypass Day or Shunt Wednesday?

And can you imagine how busy men's calendars would be if we celebrated Circumcision Day? Or would that be a day of mourning? I don't know. These things are tricky.

What I do know is that my life was not only saved one year ago but was also irrevocably changed. That surgery set in motion a chain of events that is still active and still transforming the way I look at the world—in a very positive way. Who could've known that I'd come out of abdominal surgery with better eyesight?

My friend Ray, who has been through his own battle with cancer and was always there for me throughout my adventure, once told me that he and his wife made a point of celebrating everything along the cancer journey. They celebrated getting out of the hospital, the first finished week of chemo, the second finished week of chemo, the end of chemo, the last needle and so on. I think that's a good way to go through life.

I think we could all stand to celebrate a lot more and a lot better. We need to stop and recognize milestones, however small. Make speeches, blow out candles, raise glasses. We need to keep reminding ourselves that we're winning, we're still here. And if that isn't worth celebrating, I don't know what is.

Subject: Chemo Shmemo

To: Group
From: Neil Crone
Priority: High

I was supposed to start round two of chemo today. Suz and I got down there and were stopped at the door to the oncology department and asked to put on some yellow paper mouth masks. Somebody had apparently dropped in the other day with a touch of TB. One can only marvel at the pea brain that directs somebody with TB to go into a ward full of people whose mean age is around 80 and whose collective immune systems couldn't fight off a hiccup. At any rate, we put these things on and went in. It was awful. The oncology waiting room is a sad enough place when you can actually see people's faces— it was downright horrible when you looked around and saw nothing but a sea of yellow masks and frightened eyes. Suz and I took ours off and drew smiles on the front. That helped a little.

The drill every Monday of my chemo rounds is that they first take some of my blood (I am very brave and usually get a sucker). They zip it off to the lab to make sure I don't have any tumour markers in it or Ebola or anything, and then, if all is well, they proceed with my treatments. Well, they took some blood, we waited, and then we were promptly told to go home. My white blood cell count was too low to risk another bombardment, apparently. Never thought I'd take my white blood cell count personally, but I have to tell you it's a bit of a shot to the old ego when somebody tells you you're not exactly up to snuff in the old white blood cell department. The nurse had that look on her face too, as if she was wondering what other departments I might be lacking in. I should've let her know right then and there in no uncertain terms that chemo or no chemo, Mr. Happy is still at his post, if you get my drift. I got your white blood cells right here, baby.

Anywho, we're back home. Round two is put off until next Monday— that is, providing mister sissy cells can manage to generate a few more white ones. Tomorrow we meet with my radiation doctor, Smiley. He's kind of like Ben Kingsley in *The House of Sand and Fog*—only without the humour. God knows what he'll tell us. I don't start radiation for about a month. He may just want to gently remind me once more that even with radiation my chances aren't great. He's so funny that way. We laugh and laugh. Honestly, I don't mean to generalize about oncologists, I mean they have a pretty brutal gig, but these guys really need to get out and have a few laughs. When we sit and talk with my chemo guy, it's all I can do to stop from just reaching over and giving him an atomic wedgie. Just to see his eyes light up for once. I suppose I shouldn't be so hard on them. They wallow in death all day, poor bastards. I should just give a hug when I see him. Maybe Suz could flash him. That always makes me feel a whole lot better.

On the upside, I just turned 44 on the weekend and had a wonderful time. Managed to pooch three restaurant dinners over Friday, Saturday and Sunday and only had to pay for two of them.

My birthday present arrived today as well—a brand spanking new La-Z-Boy recliner and reclining sofa. Bring on the chemo, boys, I'm lying down in style from now on. I've got things positioned perfectly so I can watch Calgary beat the snot out of Tampa tonight.

Some friends recently asked me what it is that I do with my days now that I am not really working much. It's a good question, and some days I have to ask myself, "What the hell *did* I do today?"

I generally get up with Suz and the guys, and we all have breakfast together. Well, they have breakfast—I sit there and cram gelcap after gelcap of supplements and vitamins into my mouth and wash them down with some vile good-for-my-immune-system brew that tastes like boiled gym socks. I pop more pills during a day than Keith Richards. We're seriously thinking of getting a Lazy Susan for the breakfast table just to help me keep track of which ones I've ingested and which I haven't.

Once the kids are off to school, Suzanne and I usually head into Oshawa for chemo treatments if it's that week. If not, she may head into Uxbridge to work (if I'm feeling good enough to be left to my own recognizance), and then the dog and I head out for our morning walk. I cram my pockets full of carrots and celery (all good antioxidants, you know), put on my sunglasses and floppy hat, and out we go.

We usually walk out along one of the country concession roads. It's quite lovely, this time of the year especially. I've said to Suz a bunch of times that this would be a much more difficult battle in the middle of a dreary, dark winter. As it is, we take our time, sniff every lilac bloom and apple blossom we come across and generally have a pretty darn nice time of it. I walk past the same fields and forests and river every day, but each day they look a little different. The light is different, or the crops have grown a little more or a farmer has ploughed up the earth. I never tire of it, and it always leaves me feeling wonderfully happy and positive. The other morning we almost ran smack into a bear on our walk. I've taken to wearing a whistle now. Although let's face it, no bear in his right mind would want to eat me after chemo. That'd be like having a Warfarin sandwich. That's actually one of my little amusements. Right after a full dose of chemotherapy, I'll sit out on the back deck with an arm exposed for the mosquitoes. You can actually watch them tank up on your blood, fly off and drop dead about 10 feet away. (Geez, I just reread that— I've got to get some hobbies or something.)

The rest of the day, really, is taken up with a little snoozing, a little reading, a lot of vegetable eating and some time spent on the computer writing and catching up with emails like this one. Usually I'm in the rack by 9 p.m. Not exactly Pierce Brosnan, but I'm not complaining. When things slow down like this you really do find joy and pleasure in small things. Every email I get, every note or letter or visit, is gold. Thank you all. You're keeping me connected to the rest of my world.

Well, this has gone on far too long, I'm sure. I have a La-Z-Boy to break in. Much love and health to you all.

Yours in white blood cells,

Neil

"Cancer can take away all of my
physical abilities.
It cannot touch my mind,
it cannot touch my heart,
and it cannot touch my soul."

– Jim Valvano

"You never know how
strong you are until
being strong is
the only choice you have."

– Cayla Mills

Pulp fiction helped at darkest times

Next to physical intimacy, reading has to be my favourite thing. If I could just find a way to combine the two without hurting my wife's feelings, I'd be on top of the world.

I read whenever I can. I never leave the house without a book or two stowed in my satchel or a paperback in my back pocket, and still I never have enough time to read all the books I want to. My bedside table must have a half-dozen books piled on it, all in various stages of ingestion.

I think it's important not only to read a lot but to read widely. We all know people who will only read literature. These are terribly dreary individuals who refuse to even consider a book unless someone has hanged himself in it somewhere or one or more children have died in a fire or car crash—or perhaps both. To them, a book is not worth reading unless they feel absolutely wretched upon finishing it. These people were either spanked too much or not enough as children.

I'll read anything I can get my mitts on, from Dr. Seuss to *Dr. Zhivago*. Sometimes the cheesy stuff is the best of all.

When I was laid out with cancer, I discovered pulp fiction. I would immerse myself in plots so shallow you'd scrape your knees on the first page. Books where every chapter ended with a guy hanging from a cliff or a nubile heroine surrounded by drooling maniacs or a maniac surrounded by nubile heroines. I didn't care. Those books got me through some pretty rough afternoons. They took me away.

I have friends of mine who used to pass long car trips by reading Louis L'Amour novels out loud to each other. I've tried it.

I dare anyone to read a Louis L'Amour western out loud and not be in stitches by the end of a chapter.

"Buck reached a muscled arm to take the ladle of cool well water offered by Rebecca. As the blazing sun beat hard upon the mesas, her bosom heaved."

You have to love that. As far as I'm concerned, if you can get heaving bosoms and a gunfight into the same paragraph, you're a genius.

Finally, I don't know whether it was due to improper toilet training or some festering anxiety disorder, but, for the longest time, if I started a book I had to finish it. No matter how bad the book, how much I hated it, I felt I had to read it all the way to the end.

I would lie in bed, book in hand, complaining to my wife, "Man this stinks. I can't believe how bad this is."

I would do this over and over again, sighing and shaking my head, completely ruining her own reading experience, until finally, bosom heaving, she would take the book and fling it out of my hands.

I'm better now. I have a rule. I give a book 50 pages to hook me. If I'm still struggling at that point, out it goes. Although, occasionally I'll hang onto a bad one—just to get my wife's bosom heaving. A guy's gotta have some fun.

Subject: Handing in My "Man Card"

To: Group
From: Neil Crone
Priority: High

I think I am dangerously close to having to hand in my "man card." I'll admit that I've never exactly been the poster boy for testosterone. I don't like fighting, I don't drink hard and in all of my relationships, try as I might, I always had the feeling it was me who was being deflowered. To top it all off, I became an actor. Not exactly Papa Hemingway.

But in spite of all that, I think I've managed to hang onto my maleness, if only tenuously. Lately though, with the advent of my adventures in Cancerville, I'm afraid I'm really treading on thin man-ice.

For starters, I hug everybody now. I just do. Like the newly reborn Ebenezer Scrooge, I simply can't help myself. If I liked you before, I love you now. Male friends of mine have started wearing extra layers of clothing as a buffer to my affections. But it won't stop me.

I've also developed a fondness for bath crystals and long soaks in the tub. This might not be so offensive to the members of the man guild if there was a person of the opposite gender in said tub with me. But I assure you, I'm in there alone. I like it that way. It's quiet, it's relaxing and it helps me sleep. Lately I've even started lighting candles. That, I know, is in direct contravention of Article 14, Subsection 12 of the Man Code, which specifically states that "no man shall light candles, perfumed or otherwise, in a room of bathing unless the aforementioned candles are to be used solely for either: a) establishment and proof of a 'blue angel' or b) the transparent but effective pandering to a female partner/spouse with the aim of getting lucky." The book is very clear on that.

I've also been doing yoga for over a year now, and I admit to knowing the lyrics to at least a couple of Barry Manilow songs by heart, and when I get stressed, I don't kick-box or work on my car, I bake. It's true. If you happen to drop in some time and the house smells deliciously of cookies, chances are I'm having a bad day.

Frankly, I'm tired of running. Tired of buying my shampoo in a brown paper bag, tired of sending the kids to the store to pick up some incense sticks and a tub of avocado facial scrub for the old man. Surely there have to be other men like me out there. If there are, we need to band together, to talk and share our feelings. We could meet at my place. I've just bought the most fantastic ginseng tea…

Yours with lots of hugs,

Neil

"Attitude is a little thing
that makes a big difference."

– Winston Churchill

"The human spirit is stronger than anything that can happen to it."

– C.C. Scott

Hey, Grim Reaper, take that!

I had one of those moments yesterday. You know, the ones where you very clearly feel the hand of God giving you a whack on the backside. I was on a movie set, shooting a film with Adrien Brody, Bob Hoskins and Ben Affleck—big-time Hollywood stuff.

We'd been filming for about nine or ten hours. The novelty of working with A-list stars was wearing off for everyone. It was getting very hot; the tension was getting cranked up as the day's shooting schedule appeared more and more in jeopardy. Tempers flared.

The craft table was down to wilted veggies and some unappetizing cheese stuff, and there just didn't seem to be as many comfortable chairs around as we needed. Pretty dire stuff. My back was aching because I'd been standing a lot—on account of the lack of comfy chairs. My feet were sore in my costume rental shoes, and pretty soon, as is always the case when you get two or three actors gathered together, we started griping.

I was in the middle of my fourth or fifth reiteration of how sore my feet were when I looked up and saw it. I can't explain how I hadn't seen it earlier. It clearly had been there all day long, as we were shooting right beside Lakeridge Health Oshawa. As I stood there in mid-kvetch, I found myself staring, open-mouthed, into the windows of the oncology ward. A year ago exactly, I was looking through those same windows—from the *other* side.

It hit me like a hammer to the side of the head. The windows are tinted, but I could still make out the chairs, those big, vinyl reclining chairs lined up around the periphery of the room, each one holding a tired, frightened soul.

The world stood very still for me then.

I could no longer hear the whining going on around me or the clinking, clanking buzz of the film set. The only sound I heard was my own heart beating heavily in my throat. I watched the shadows of nurses moving busily from chair to chair, dispensing hope, while the Grim Reaper leaned patiently against the outside wall, bony arms crossed, a cigarette dangling from his grey lips. He looked over at me and winked.

Suddenly, I wanted to cross the street. I wanted to push him out of the way, rush into the cancer ward in my makeup and costuming and shout, "Look! Look! It's me! I was here. I was one of you! But I'm OK now. I'm better! You will be too! I swear you will."

And in that instant, just when I thought my heart would burst through my chest, I was swept back to the present. And, like Saul on the road to Damascus, I opened my eyes and saw the world around me once more with perfect clarity. I felt like Scrooge waking up and finding out he has not missed Christmas morning.

I shut my mouth, smiled hugely at my complaining companions and walked—no, *skipped*—over to the craft table for some delicious veggies and cheese. Then I sat down on the grass, the beautifully cool green grass. I closed my eyes and, tilting my idiotic face heavenward, said a quiet "Thank you."

Subject: Learning to Say No

To: Group
From: Neil Crone
Priority: High

One of the cardinal rules that was indelibly tattooed on my soul during my training as an improviser is to always say "Yes." Basically, this means never, ever, on pain of death, negate or block an idea or offer given to you. On stage it can lead to hilarity. I walk into a scene, for example, thinking I'm going to be a pirate, when, before I can utter a "Yar" or a "Shiver me timbers," another performer walks onstage and says to me, "G'day Mrs. O'Reilly! And how is that gout of yours doin'?" As a performer trained from birth to say "Yes" to anything and everything, I don't flip out or try to push my pirate idea into the scene. Instead, if I know what's good for me, I happily shift gears, chucking Bluebeard out the window to become a gout-ridden (and potentially entertaining) Irish washerwoman. The point is to get into the frame of mind where your first reaction, always, is to throw positive energy behind ideas—not shutting them down or naysaying. More than just a useful rule for performers, it's a marvellous way to go through life.

That's why I'm having a difficult time learning to say "No" all of a sudden. As a result of my introduction to Cancer Man and his annoying sidekick, Chemo-sah-bee, I have had to take a pass on a lot of things that used to bring me a great deal of pleasure. Things that defined a big part of who I was. I cannot coach my son's softball team. I cannot help my wonderful friends snatch defeat from the jaws of victory in our annual beach volleyball tournament. I cannot swim in the lake at the cottage. I cannot lose myself in a blissful hour of stopping or not stopping pucks on a Thursday night with the boys. I cannot ride my bike until I feel my heart kicking wildly and joyously in my throat. I cannot perform. One by one, I have had to say a regretful "No" to these and other activities that I once embraced with a hearty improviser's "Yes!" It has been difficult and it has made me, in turn, angry, sad and self-pitying.

But just lately (I am a slow learner after all) I am beginning to realize that no matter how many "No's" one has to spit out, there are always things to still say "Yes" to. As I write this, for instance, I am sitting, comfortably ensconced in a pile of cushions, on my screened-in balcony, surrounded by an orchestra of birdsong and the lush green wallpaper of a maple tree—my dog happily lazing beside me. It is quite magical. Had I not had to learn to say "No" to all of those other things, I might never have thought to say "Yes" to this. Another gift from Cancer Man? I'm not sure. I'm still not returning the jerk's calls. Hopefully, though, when all of this is done and I have thrown away all memory of torment and needles and sickness, I will have retained this simple yet extraordinary ability to always look for the thing to say "Yes" to. Try it yourself. I think you'll find it's a lifesaver.

Yours,

Neil

"Hope is the physician
of each misery."

– Irish Proverb

"We cannot direct the wind,
but we can adjust the sails."

– Anonymous

Survivors and spouses share stories

I just spent a remarkable weekend with a friend I hardly know, and yet who I am intimately close to.

We have only really met three times, yet we are, in a sense, like brother and sister.

We come from widely divergent backgrounds and upbringings. We live in very different settings, but we have one very critical bond. Gill is two years in remission from lymphoma. I am almost one year in remission from colon cancer.

Like war veterans or plane crash survivors, we speak the same secret language—a language punctuated with immense joy and relief but also with its share of guilt and fear. Both of us have watched friends and loved ones fight and lose battles with cancer while we, somehow, continued on. Both of us have revelled in glorious days of borrowed time, and

both of us have felt an icy finger down our spines while nervously awaiting CT scan or scope results. Both of us are trying like hell to live and love like there's no tomorrow while working very hard not to think about the possibility of no tomorrow. It's a weird balancing act.

So being together to talk and hug and laugh and cry was a very good thing. It was also a very good thing for our spouses. Cancer has long fingers, and it profoundly touches anyone who comes near it. Caregivers have their own unique needs and burdens, carrying the combined weight of the sick and the healthy in the family—and always with a worried eye on a future alone.

It was therefore lovely and comforting to see my Suzanne and Gill's Gord instantly connecting and easily sharing so much. At one magical point during our first evening together, the four of us were sitting out on the screened-in porch of Gill and Gord's cottage. Gill and I were engaged in a passionate discussion about some aspect of our adventures when I stopped for a moment and realized that Suzanne and Gord were in the middle of an equally important and probably very similar dialogue. There was some serious healing going on out on that porch.

And that was largely how the weekend went.

We swam and ate and laughed and played with the children, and very often we talked about those things that un-cancered people talk about—the weather, our kids, books, our kids. But always and eventually, the conversational compass point drifted back to what had drawn the four of us together in the first place.

I'm not a big support group kind of guy. I'm sure they do marvellous things for a lot of people, but I've never really been comfortable in that atmosphere.

But with Gill and Gord and Suzanne, it's different. It's four people happily hanging onto one another. It's the shared message that it's OK to be scared, but it feels better to be happy. It's survivors speaking the same language.

To: Group
From: Neil Crone
Priority: High

I have a million cards in my wallet. Credit cards, debit cards, library cards, book club cards, organ donor cards, baseball cards—as I said, a lot of cards. Some are more useful than others, but there are a couple in there that just make me shake my head. Do you know that I actually have a cancer card? I do. I'm not really sure why, but I have one. Every time I go to the hospital for chemotherapy I have to present my card at the front desk. This is undoubtedly an effort to thwart crooks coming into the hospital and getting somebody else's chemo. I guess that happens a lot. Chemo junkies walking in off the street and pretending to be sick so they can get their fix. Boy, that's when you know you've really hit rock bottom.

I know there are very real reasons for keeping meticulous track of the info on that card, and I am glad they do it; but it still makes me giggle. Believe me, a card is the last thing you need to tell if someone is getting chemo. Look at their eyes, look at their hair, look at their spirit; those'll tell the story every time.

The radiation people are equally canny. You can't just sneak into Sunnybrook and wheedle your way into a free radiation tan, my friend. They're tough. Before letting you into the room they ask you tricky questions like "What is your birthday?" or "What's your middle name?" And even if you should somehow bluff your way through that checkpoint, there's no getting around the final qualifier. Once you're on the table they haul your drawers down and check your heinie for their special tattoos. I think they got that idea from the Illuminati. Anyway, I'm tempted, one of these nights, to give them the wrong answer, or ink in some new butt tattoos of my own, just to see what would happen. I imagine flashing lights coming on, blaring claxons and burly radiation cops giving me the bum's rush out of there. Come to think of it, maybe that wouldn't be so bad.

The other perplexing card that I carry around with me is a catheter ID card, an indispensable little item that instantly alerts anyone I care to show it to that I have a tube sticking out of my arm. I can't tell you how many times a day I have to flash this baby. "Neil, could you cut the lawn?" Flash. "Neil could you take the garbage out?" Flash. "Neil could you…" Flash. It comes in pretty handy.

I think what I hate most about these cards, as with the medical gauze arm band I perpetually wear around (to hold in place the tube sticking out of my arm), is that they are a constant, unwelcome reminder that I am not entirely healthy. That something is wrong at some level. But guess what? I know that. And I spend untold amounts of energy putting myself in a happy mindset so I can deal with it. I don't need a freaking card to remind me.

With gratitude,

Neil

"Optimism is the foundation of courage."

– Nicholas Murray Butler

"Some days there
won't be a song in your heart.
Sing anyway."

– Emory Austin

Saying goodbye to an old acquaintance

I closed a long open chapter of a difficult book yesterday. After spending the weekend with my brothers and my dad, playing poker and closing up the cottage, I drove back with an old acquaintance sitting in the back seat—my brother J.J.'s aluminum walker. After a battle with liver cancer, J.J. died in June 1982, just six days shy of his 24th birthday.

A few months before his death he had begun to use a walker to help him get around. Always an athletic, supremely independent individual, he hated it. We hated it too, for the 23 years it hung in the rafters of the cottage garage. It was, for me and I am sure many others, an ugly symbol of an ugly time. I couldn't look at it, for even the briefest glimpse, without a tide of sadness washing over me.

I can't imagine what kind of relationship my father, who spent so much time in that garage, had with it. I suspect the only reason it was kept around at all was because he had used it. For all of its dark mojo, it was still a tie to J.J., and as the years pass and the rest of our lives unfold, those ties become more tenuous and precious. We are loath to release them, however misshapen.

But this summer my dad seemed ready to let it go. Ironically, it did not seem to want to go. He had tried to lose it in a series of yard sales, but like something out of a work by Poe, it kept hanging around. Like some four-legged poltergeist, it steadfastly remained while the tools and the knick-knacks and the fondue sets went off with strangers. Perhaps it had developed an affinity for us and the melancholy it brought into our lives.

When I pulled up to the cottage on Saturday, it was the first thing I saw—sitting out in the drizzle and the cold, basking in misery, happy as a clam. I think that was when I'd had enough. Suddenly I couldn't wait to be shut of the damned thing. I tore its leg extensions off, stuffed it into the car, then walked down to the cottage.

It was waiting for me when it was time to go. It sat in the backseat and glared at me in the rear-view mirror the whole way home. It seemed to laugh at me. It knew all about my own health issues. It knew all about my fears. It couldn't wait to tell me all about how my brother had suffered. It thought I was taking it home.

I did take it home—I took it to a long-term care facility. I took it to a place where it was no big deal—nothing special, just another piece of equipment, no better than a commode—a place where it wasn't going to scare anybody anymore. You should have heard it squeal as I dropped it off among a pile of other walkers and canes. That was the first time in 23 years that I was able to look at that thing and laugh.

Subject: My Stay at the Hospital

To: Group
From: Neil Crone
Priority: High

Day 1: I awake in the recovery room, not sure who I am, but I figure I must be a fighter pilot whose plane went down. I am wearing an oxygen mask. Someone is torturing me by grinding his heel into my bladder. A voice, cleverly disguised as friendly, reassures me it is only the discomfort of a catheter I am feeling. "Right, comrade," I mumble through my air hose, you're not getting jack outta me, Mr. Ho Chi Minh. Not for all the tea in...

Suddenly I am moving. Lights are flashing by overhead and I am banged and jostled as we play chicken with other gurneys, medical carts and walls. There is lots of laughter, all of it female. I must've said something funny. I am a freaking hoot.

I am taken to my room. Partition curtains are swept back and there is much chatter and bustle and cranking of levers. "Mr. Crone, we're just going to transfer you onto your bed. Can you help us out here?"

"Sure, no sweat, just as soon as this gorilla gets off my chest."

Nurses come and go, pleasant and efficient and kind and funny. Prodding and poking, and always leaving the sad sack of pain feeling more human than he surely must look. And underneath all of this, the blissfully cool touch of loved ones' hands across the scorched hardpan of my forehead.

Day 2, 3, 4, 5 (who can tell anymore, morphine has arrived…):
I have a morphine pain pump. It looks like a toy. The Fisher-Price Pump'n Play. Morphine is my friend. I squeeze my pump and the gorilla goes away. Unfortunately, no matter how many times I squeeze my pump it cannot make my roommate go away. I call him Lou, because he is a lunatic. I don't think Lou has a gorilla on his chest. He is far too active for that. But I am beginning to think he has a monkey on his back. Lou does amusing things like pull his IV out so he can go have a smoke. He calls the nurses bad names and swears at himself all night long. He puts all the lights on at night and runs back and forth in his wheelchair, smacking the foot of my bed with each passing. Lou is more fun than TV. But I don't want fun. I want to sleep. The gorilla wants fun. I don't say anything to Lou. Partly because I am a morphine-soaked, titanium-stapled lump—and partly because I feel sorry for him. But then, Lou crosses the line. I open my eyes in panic one night. It sounds like there is a fire in my room. I push the gorilla over a bit so I can look around. What I mistook for the sound of flames is the crinkling of Cellophane. Lou, nocturnal as a wombat, is at the foot of my bed going through my fruit basket. I shout at him to beat it and frantically hammer the nurse call button like an angry senior at a crosswalk. The nurses come. They are righteously pissed at Lou. Maybe they will yank his catheter out or something. I would stay up to watch that. Instead, Lou is restrained and I am moved to a private room. Sorry Lou, I know we're each dealing with our own personal primates, but nobody touches my fruit basket.

Love,

Neil

"There is no hope unmingled with fear, no fear unmingled with hope."

– Baruch Spinoza

"Courage is not the absence of fear, but rather the judgment that something else is more important than fear."

– Ambrose Redmoon

Cherish every moment on this earth

One of the weird habits I've picked up since going through my dance with cancer has been that every Saturday morning, along with my coffee and the pleasant, chatty company of my wife and kids, I spend a few moments glancing through the obituary section of the paper. I don't know precisely when or even why I started doing this, but at some point over the last three years it has become a routine— and a surprisingly pleasant one at that.

Far from creepy or morose, the feeling that I get as I look at the faces, young and old, of the recently deceased is remarkably warm and fuzzy. It is as though each one of them, along with the often heartbreaking messages from the families they've left behind, is reminding me in the most profound way of the im-

portance of each day, each hour, each second we draw breath.

Staring down the barrel of my own demise several years ago was infinitely life altering. I am forever grateful for the life lessons my ugly little friend, cancer, taught me. However, like all human beings I tend to be forgetful. Three years clear of a cancer diagnosis, I find myself falling into some troubling old patterns. Worry, fear, boredom and a dozen other equally vile little germs have been cropping up as regularly as in the good old days. Days when I thought I would live forever, when I took my time here for granted.

The obits can be a neat little inoculation against such viruses. Each grainy black and white photograph, each life boiled down to a paragraph and the stark finality of each birth and death date cut very cleanly to the heart of the matter. We are here for a very short time indeed. Let us not waste a second of it.

Instead, let us stop and look around us, eyes wide, at the blessings and love and joy that are ours for the taking. Let us be still occasionally and listen to the voices of the dead pleading with us to savour it all—the good, the bad, the easy, the hard, the cold and the warm. Life.

One of my favourite sayings came from legendary rocker Warren Zevon who, only months before his death from mesothelioma, the same cancer that killed Steve McQueen, told David Letterman and millions of viewers to "Enjoy every sandwich."

Amen.

So simple but right on the money.

I hope you'll do yourself a favour this year and forget about losing weight or getting fit or writing that novel. Instead, do two simple things that I guarantee will change your life in a million wonderful ways.

Spend a few minutes listening in the obituary section every Saturday morning, and tape the words "Enjoy every sandwich" up on every mirror in your house. If you can make yourself slow down, even a little, you'll give all the great things in your life the chance to catch up with you.

Soon you'll be awash in them. I wish you all the blessings in the world. Happy New Year.

Subject: Rectum? Darn Near Killed 'im

To: Group
From: Neil Crone
Priority: High

I'm still here. Sorry for the delay since my last communication but I've just not been up to it. I think (he said cautiously) that I have finally turned a corner on this thing. It was touch and go there for a while, though, believe me. Another few days of radiation and chemo and I would've talked. I would've sung my head off, told those bastards everything they wanted to know. Studio locations, actors who were still in the closet, even Colin Mochrie's home phone number. I was that close to cracking.

Radiation ended just over a week ago and I got the PICC line out of my arm a few days later. Suzanne and I were pulling our hair out as we waited forever at the hospital to get rid of the chemo pump. We couldn't get the damned thing out of there fast enough, but we had to wait hours it seemed. You'd think that after six weeks another couple of hours wouldn't be a big deal. But I could taste freedom, and I desperately wanted it. The truly stupid thing was that at the last moment my oncologist suggested that I leave the PICC line in. She said it would make my future chemo injections much easier. Easier for whom? Let's just do the math on that one for a moment. I can either wear the PICC for what would amount to another three months (no showers, no swimming, no sleeveless gowns) or endure the momentary pain of four more short injections in the hand? Hmmm. That's a toughie. I felt like telling her, "You wear one of these pricks for close to five months, and you tell me what you'd rather do?" I wanted it out, and I wanted it out now. I just wanted to feel a little human again. To walk around and not see the eyes of everyone I meet dart to the hideous tube sticking out of my arm. To not have a constant reminder that I am not well. Anyway, it came out. And I couldn't be happier.

So I'm at the family cottage for the next little while. My parents, bless them, have made the place available to Suz and the boys and me for as long as we need it. I'm nowhere near normal yet, my life is still on a tether with one end tied to a toilet seat, and I'm still pretty much on a diet of Cream of Wheat and Wonder Bread with a yogourt chaser, but each day I think I am a little better. Fewer cramps and more energy. I actually went snorkelling with my sons the other day. That rocked. Although I've got so little body fat left (there's still a small deposit between my ears apparently) that I get really cold very quickly.

Can't tell you how hard that last five weeks was. I don't think I was mentally prepared for it. Frankly I don't know how you could be. It's different for everybody I guess. Each nightly drive down to Sunnybrook was, quite literally, a crapshoot. We were never sure if my hair-trigger colon wanted to play games or not. If we had a 6 p.m. departure time, I generally had to eat dinner around 4 o'clock to give me a couple of hours flow-through time. We also stowed a four-quart Tupperware container in the backseat, for, well, containing stuff. Amazingly, I was caught short only once, making a mad dash into the woods just west of Leaskdale. On the upside, Suzanne is now able to safely operate a vehicle in excess of 150 km/h. By the way, why is it that when you really have to crap you inevitably get stuck behind a pair of seniors out poking around for a fresh berry stand?

Anyway, if anybody out there was frightened or caused any undue stress by a yellow VW Bug illegally streaking past them on a double line with oodles of oncoming traffic, we apologize.

Suzanne continues to be Wonder Woman, keeping the house and the kids together and still looking after a pathetic husband who is at his worst—a whining 44-year-old in diapers who won't eat his vegetables. She has so far administered almost 60 injections, most of which hurt her a lot more than they hurt me. Thankfully she always kisses the boo-boo. Most doctors won't do that.

So, here we are. I have four weeks off before my second-last round of chemo begins. They said that it would more than likely be a couple of weeks before the side effects really abated, and it looks (and feels) like we're on that schedule. I'm really hoping that by the end of this month-long sabbatical, I'll be eating fruit and veggies again—and maybe even a hamburger or two. I can dream, can't I?

The last two chemo treatments will be like the first ones I received—a visit each day to the hospital for a week where I sit in a chair and get an injection of goodies. I know what to expect from these ones now. Not fun, but not the marathon of the five-week trots. I can handle a little nausea and the odd mouth sore. It's really not much different from gonorrhea. And who hasn't been there?

If all goes to schedule, we'll be wrapped up by just after Thanksgiving. In the meantime, as always, thank you all from the bottom of my colon for your support and email check-ins. I've been in a weird position over the last couple of months—desperately lonely at times, but usually too tired or too embarrassed to entertain company. Many nights—nights when I could not sleep and was tired of the idiocy of late-night television, and haunted by being the only one awake in a sleeping household—I would turn on the computer and read and reread your letters. (By the way, is there anything worse than a sleeping household when you are the only one up, alone with your discomfort?)

The lifeline was always there, and I was always very grateful to grab hold. Thanks heaps everyone, you're lifesavers, every one of you.

Hopefully the next letter will be faster in coming and will hold much nicer news. Until then, much love to you all.

I think of you often,

Neil

"Cancer taught me to stop saving things for a special occasion. Every day is special. You don't have to get cancer to start living life to the fullest. My post-cancer philosophy? No wasted time. No ugly clothes. No boring movies."

– Regina Brett

"The wish for healing has always been half of health."

– Lucius Annaeus Seneca

Bracelet a reminder of what is important

I have a silver bracelet that is very important to me. I don't really like wearing a bracelet. I've never really considered myself a bracelet kind of guy. Bracelet guys have always been like necklace guys in my books. They drive snazzy cars and wear loads of cologne. They get married a lot—mostly to women with winter tans and names like Crystal, Tiffany or Chantal, women who dig snazzy cars and cologne. I could never pull that off. I don't think women named Crystal, Tiffany or Chantal dig guys who flood rinks and kiss their dogs on the lips.

I know that my own wife, whose name is nowhere close to Crystal or any other mineral, kind of hates my bracelet. She knows it's important to me, though, and bites her tongue. She's a good friend. Still, I'm fairly sure there would be an immediate and frank discussion if I ever came home in a snazzy car or came downstairs reeking of something called Bilge pour l'homme.

My bracelet is important because it is a reminder. On it are written seven words that have become lifesavers for me: "Nothing is worth more than this day." That's it. That's all. "Nothing is worth more than this day."

Each morning when I get up and get dressed, regardless of what worry or issue or concern is careening around inside my head, when I reach for this silver bracelet I am reminded to put the brakes on for just a moment and realign my attitude for the day.

I am reminded that I had cancer and am still here and that others are not. I am reminded to take a look around me at my warm house, my soft bed, my warm, soft wife, my beautiful children and all the million things waiting to be enjoyed in this day I've just been given.

You might find it hard to believe that someone who has had a life-threatening disease could ever forget to be in love with this precious thing called existence. But it happens.

You get better, your hair grows back and you put your toes into the stream of life once more. If you're not really strong on your feet, however, you soon find yourself swiftly sucked along by the same old current of worry, fear and pettiness that defined your existence prior to your tumour. I think it's called human nature.

I wish it were human nature for all of us to awaken each day thrilled with its possibilities and delights, eager and excited to embrace the joy awaiting us. But it is not. At least not in my neck of the woods. Instead, most of us need a reminder.

There may have been a time in our rural past when we awakened and walked outside to be greeted by the glory of nature. The beauty of the fields, flowers, woods and sky loudly proclaimed how precious the day was. But most of us have a difficult time finding enlightenment in the glow of the TV or the dashboard lights or the arlarm clock LED blinking 5 a.m. Hence, the bracelet.

You may not want to be a bracelet guy. I'd understand if you didn't. There are only so many Tiffanys and Chantals to go round, after all. Still, I hope you can find something somewhere that will spark you to reset your compass every morning. It's made all the difference in the world to me. And it's cheaper than cologne.

Subject: Recalled to Hockey

To: Group
From: Neil Crone
Priority: High

I'm about to start playing hockey again—another week or so. I love the game. I used to look forward to my hockey nights all week long. So, you think I'd be very excited. But, quite frankly, I'm terrified. It's been almost a year since I put on the "tools of ignorance," as they say in the goaltending trade. Not a huge span of time in the big picture; however, in the world of pickup hockey, when you're 44, that's a lifetime. Luckily, I numbered my equipment after I took it off last time, so I'll know where everything goes when I put it back on again. And it's not my conditioning that I'm concerned about so much either. To tell the truth, I was in better shape than some of the guys I've played with when I was lying in a hospital bed with a belly full of staples. No, it's more of a mental thing, really. I mean, I haven't played in almost a year.

I shouldn't get so worked up, I suppose. I'm sure it's probably just like sex or riding a bike. Once you do it, you never forget how. Of course I'd feel a hell of a lot better if I'd had sex or ridden a bike in the past year, too.

I know that, if I have a bad first outing, I can always play the cancer card, and nobody's going to say anything. But I won't be able to hide behind that for long. A hockey dressing room is like a really smelly version of the Spanish Inquisition. Those guys are merciless. And the more they love you, the harder they are on you. Even after my best games—games when I stood on my head—I'd still get nailed with a bucket of friendly ridicule. And when I think about it, I wouldn't have it any other way. If you're not getting your share of abuse in a dressing room, Sheldon Kennedy aside, you're not really a part of the team. Guys don't hug or give effusive praise. If you've played well or if the herd accepts you, you get made fun of. How you take that ridicule tells the group a lot about you.

So, I guess, more than anything else, what I'm afraid of at the end of that first game back—when the jerseys come off and the beer gets opened and the showers fill the air with steam—is silence. Silence would be very bad. Silence means "You stunk, but you had cancer so we're not gonna say anything" or "Wow. We thought you might be a little rusty, but what the hell was that?" or worse, "Man, I wonder if they got all his tumour out?" I think I could handle playing badly and getting razzed. I could certainly handle playing well and getting razzed. But not getting anything would be upsetting. As a matter of fact, I don't think I'll really feel fully at ease until that first insult. Then I'll know for sure that I'm safely back among friends.

With appreciation,

Neil

"Don't miss your life."

– Valerie Harper

"Cancer didn't bring me
to my knees,
it brought me to my feet."
– Michael Douglas

Friend's email brings response of love

I met Andrew and his lovely wife, Marilyn, a couple of years ago at a cancer fundraiser. I had noticed this tall, completely bald guy making a lot of people laugh throughout the evening. I was hosting—you get to see a lot from up there at the podium. He seemed like an interesting guy, even from up there. Later on I got a closer look and I noticed, for the first time, the large scars and slight indentations on Andrew's skull. This gentleman is intimately acquainted with surgery, I thought. At any rate, we were— through thought or design, fate or the finger of God—brought together and by night's end had made plans to meet again.

That's the way it often is in the cancer community. People don't waste time. There's not a lot of pussyfooters in the cancer world.

Life is precious.

I discovered how very precious life is to my friend Andrew.

Here is a guy who has had, over a number of procedures, a very large chunk of his brain removed in a constant battle with cancer. And yet he, with approximately half his normal grey matter, is in my humble opinion, smarter than the leader of the United States. Andrew has been on more varieties of chemo than I can count. His bloodstream is like the Baskin-Robbins of chemo. He has also outlived every dire prognosis given him. Statistics and current medical wisdom had him dead a couple of years ago. But he is still here, and he is very much alive. He burns with life. He is a neat guy to stand beside. You can feel the heat.

So when I received what was for Andrew and his normally remarkably upbeat manner a decidedly sad email, my heart broke. He has run out of his 31 flavours. There is no more chemo left to try, and the cancer is growing. They are taking him off it. He has been told that his death is not imminent—but, as my dad says, "I wouldn't order any soft-boiled eggs."

Andrew has had to arrange palliative care, make his own funeral arrangements and explain to his two tearful, angry children what is happening—all without coming completely undone himself.

I had cancer once, a very bad cancer. I looked down that black barrel a couple of times, but I was spared seeing the bullet with my name on it. I never got to the point where someone finally put a timetable on my life, where I went shopping for tombstones and epitaphs, where I envisioned, I mean really saw, my kids without a dad. Andrew is there.

But, typically, he is there with his usual faith, courage, love and depthless humour. My overwhelming emotion upon receiving his email, besides a terrible heartache, was love. I was swallowed by love—my love for him and his family, and greater still, the enormity of love that I knew was required for him to pen those hard, painful words to me.

And as hard as they are to read, they are a gift—a mighty gift. You put those words in your head, words from someone who is seeing the world and the beauty of it as clearly as anyone ever saw it, and your own vision crisps up considerably. That kind of gift has an enormous price tag. Thank you for that, Andrew—and for so much more, my friend.

Subject: Report from Cancer Central

To: Group
From: Neil Crone
Priority: High

Let me begin this missive by thanking each and every one of you for reading all of this type. It occurred to me, as I was adding all of your names to the bcc list of this letter, what an incredible number of good, patient friends I have. This really means so much to me. An opportunity to communicate and to share some of this gunk with others makes it all a lot more bearable, believe me. So, once more, thanks everyone.

I am currently in the first leg of the hump. The five-week odyssey of constant chemo infusion and nightly radiation treatments. The radiation ends each week on Friday, but the chemo, God love it, works overtime, 24/7. The little bastard's like some owner of a corner store.

I wear a pump now. It's a little electronic box about the size of a large cellphone or maybe one of those Texas Instruments calculators we used to cheat our way through Calculus back in the 70s. It lives in a fanny pack around my waist. It has an official name, the CADD Prizm 240 or something like that. I've had it on for five days now, though, and as we've gotten to know one another I'm realizing that CADD Prizm 240 just doesn't work. It's far too impersonal. After all, I sleep with this thing, bathe with this thing, move my bowels with this thing—I think we should at least be on a first name basis. So, I'm trying different handles out. So far I've got "Grendel," "Gollum,"

"Beelzebub" and, oh yeah, "Brad." I'll let you know which one sticks as I try them out over the next five weeks.

The pump thing really isn't all that much of a hassle. Believe it or not, you do acclimatize yourself fairly quickly to having an extra appendage. I probably wouldn't even realize it was there most of the time except that it makes this angry little growl every 15 minutes or so when it pushes another toxic load into my bloodstream. It actually sounds like it's enjoying itself. The little shit. I've taken to stuffing it under a pillow at night so Suz and I don't have to listen to it.

I have home-care nurses who come on a weekly basis and flush out my PICC line and change my dressing. They are wonderful people, all of them very funny and energetic. More like friends than medical staff, they are very helpful with any questions or fears I might have. One of them even told me where babies come from. Wow, was that icky.

The radiation treatments are a different deal altogether. Imagine making a nightly appointment to go into a room, lie down in front of complete strangers and stick your bare ass up in the air. I know some of you are remembering a distant trip to Thailand and nodding your heads. I'm gonna be 99 years old, and I'm still going to have nightmares in which I hear that cold, flat, disembodied voice saying, "OK now, Mr. Crone, I'm just going to put this piece of metal by your anus…OK?"

How do you respond to that? "Hey, no worries, Chu, my anus is your anus, pal."

The worst part is trying to make small talk with your face jammed down through a rubber hole in the table while some technician is shoving your hips around like a slab of fresh salmon. Thankfully, the whole thing really only takes about 15 minutes, so I just remember my days in prison and breathe through it.

Probably the hardest part of this step in the journey is that they've been more than upfront in telling me that the worst is yet to come. Apparently around the two-week mark, as a result of the combination of chemo and radiation, I may experience anything from mild diarrhea to spontaneous combustion. I can't wait.

Meantime, I confess I am very tired most of the time. And that's starting to bug me. Maybe it's just because I'm in the middle of this thing and the end seems a long ways away, or maybe I'm just sick of being sick. Whatever the reason, I find my patience is easily taxed. I find myself sliding quickly into sarcasm—a nasty yet sometimes pleasurable place to be.

Suzanne is still my greatest friend and helper. Can't imagine where I would be without her. Probably on a float in the Pride Parade or something. I don't know. She shows remarkable patience and love every day. I know I'm not the easiest guy to live with on some days. And she is carrying not only my worries but her own and those of the kids as well. To top things off, I have asked her if she can hold the pump while we have sex. That may have been a bad call.

Anyway my friends, here we are, in the middle of this goofiness. On my good days, I do feel quite well and am genuinely happy to be here and know that it will all end very shortly. On those dark days, though—days when it seems like it's all caving in on me, when tears are a blink away—I take great comfort in knowing how many of you are out there sending help. You're my salvation at those times. You really are. As I've said before, and I will say again and again and again, please keep those cards and letters coming, folks. They're the rope I'm clinging to.

Heaps of love to you all,

Neil

"You have to fight through some bad days to earn the best days of your life."

– Author Unknown

"Courage does not always roar.
Sometimes courage
is the quiet voice at the end of
the day saying, 'I will try again
tomorrow.'"

– Mary Anne Radmacher

Words of comfortable wisdom

Might as well get comfortable. I came across this phrase recently, and for some reason, it has stuck with me. It's been rattling around my head for a few days, trying to get my attention. Might as well get comfortable. I like it. Seems like something I'd like to get tattooed on me somewhere. That is, if I were comfortable getting tattooed.

Like a lot of simple but important statements, there's more going on here than first meets the eye. Life, I think most of us would agree, can be challenging—even difficult at times. Throw in a cold, dark, icy winter and it can seem downright daunting. So, what's a person to do? Well, might as well get comfortable.

If we stopped, took a moment—at the beginning of every day, or at the onset of any chore, project or responsibility, or in the face of any difficulty or trial—and pon-dered that simple phrase *might as well get comfortable*, I wonder what effect it might have?

Might as well get comfortable. Might as well find something to like here, something to take the edge off, something to sneak a little peace in with. In other words, how can we lace our day with stuff that makes us feel better? That makes life more enjoyable and less of a struggle? What little or large thing can we do to tip the scales of our present moment over into happiness? How do we keep our vibe purring at a higher frequency?

Might as well get comfortable. Again, it doesn't sound too terribly important, but it is. If you're reading this, you're alive. You're here. And like all the rest of us, you have a plate in front of you that, more than likely, has a lot of stuff on it. Some of it you love, some of it you don't care for quite so much. Some of it you placed there yourself. Some of it was dished out by somebody or something else. And every morning, when you haul yourself out of bed and place your tired feet on the floor, you have a choice. You get to decide how you're going to deal with what's on your plate. You may not like it, but at the risk of sounding like Yoda, deal with it you must. Might I suggest, you might as well get comfortable.

I like to think that the universe is designed in such a way that, at any given time, there are options available to all of us. What, after all, does our day consist of but a series of decisions and choices? Sausage or bacon? Anger or laughter? Thong or commando? Therefore, isn't a large part of how that day unfolds, comfortably or uncomfortably, up to us and what we choose?

If I should find myself suffocating in traffic gridlock, last in line at the checkout behind a guy with a jar of pennies, sucking wind at the bottom of the driveway as the plow seals me in yet again…I could blow a panel, lose it, hit the roof. But really, I might as well just get comfortable. I might as well find something redeeming, halfway pleasant or, at the very least, funny about the situation.

The longer I'm here, the more I'm aware of how terrifyingly fast it all goes by. And how criminal it is to waste even a second of it in misery, anger or negativity. I deserve better and so do you. So, might as well get comfortable. What do you say?

Subject: The Real Story

To: Group
From: Neil Crone
Priority: High

Well, I'm back. After a week and a half of not being able to work a computer mouse without breaking into a sweat or passing out from exhaustion, I'm finally able to sit at the keyboard and get back in touch with my friends.

Let's see, where to begin? It's all been such fun. Chemo is everything they say it is—and less. Were it not for the nurses constantly coming on to me, I'm not sure I'd like to go back. Suzanne has been very good about their sexual advances, though, and bravely turns a blind eye. She is only thinking of my health. What a trooper.

For those of you who have not been through or known someone going through cancer treatment, it may be mildly beneficial for me to give you the abridged version. Everyone is different of course, but in my case it is sort of like having a mild flu all the time. You just feel really off. For most of the past week and a half, I have been very tired all of the time and mildly nauseous, my mouth sometimes inexplicably tasting like I've brushed my teeth with Brasso. I'm lucky, though. I've not actually been sick to my stomach. It's really more like if you had to watch continuous reruns of *Who's the Boss?* or *Full House*—that kind of nausea.

A very weird side effect that we had read about but had not anticipated was how nasty the sun will be to me. In a mere five minutes, I got badly burned just standing outside the car park by the hospital waiting for Suz to bring the car around.

Consequently, I bought a couple of big floppy-brimmed hats. I now look like Truman Capote on steroids, as I walk around in my long cotton sleeves, hat and sunglasses.

I've had to contend with a few blisters on my lips (again, another expected side effect of the chemo), but it really hasn't been too bad. I've heard horror stories from other people whose mouths were covered in them. Karma is being kinder to me than I deserve, I guess.

There has been one other unexpected side effect, which has been a little shocking. I'm just going to have to learn to live with enormous genitals, I guess. Who knew?

Suz and I continue to read and educate ourselves about this business. Our attitudes toward it all have changed, matured if you will. We've gone from being sad and frightened to taking a much more businesslike approach. We have a job to do, and the job will take about five to six months. Then we will be done. It will be difficult at times—at times uncomfortable—but there is a limit to it. I look forward to my son's 13th birthday at the end of September. Then this will all be a memory.

I miss a lot of you. Some of you I don't—you know who you are. I miss being more human and not looking sick. I'm at the point where I rip off bandages and cotton swabs covering up my needle holes simply because I think they make me look, and therefore feel, sick. I want to wrestle with my children again, and I think I will soon. Today, as you can tell perhaps by my long-windedness at the keyboard, is a turning point. I feel better. More like me.

I am not working, acting that is. I don't know that I will be able to this summer. The three weeks of recovery time in between treatments doesn't give you much space to book and do a gig. And in a month or so, I'm looking at five solid weeks of continuous chemo and radiation every day. I don't think I'll have much strength or time then to do anything more than glow in the dark. I'm writing, though. Thank God for writing. I'm hoping to start my second book this summer. That is a goal to focus on.

But I am planning on coming back—back to work, back to Toronto, back to my wonderfully creative, wonderfully funny actor friends, back to my hockey buddies, back to my neighbours and family, and back to my life. Things have just been postponed for a while.

In the meantime, I am taking all of this as a gift. If that sounds funny, let me explain. Imagine if you woke up one day and were suddenly vividly and deliriously aware of how much love there was surrounding you at every turn of your life? Imagine being able to fall in love all over again and in a much stronger way with your spouse and to love and cherish your children and friends as you never before thought possible? And all you had to do was go through a few months of discomfort? That's kind of where I'm at—and I'm realizing it's not really a bad place to be. Just a different place.

I want to thank you all for helping me get to that place. Your kindness and support and love have been the signposts directing me along the way.

I still have my days, of course—and Suzie will be the first to tell you this—where I think I've been dealt a shitty hand and I'm in a pissy, petulant mood, but I'm getting better at dealing with those. Meditation is a wonderful thing.

In the interim, thanks once more dear friends and family for everything. I love you all tremendously. Take good care and eat your fucking broccoli.

Your dear friend,

Neil

"Believe in who you are,
believe in what you feel,
your power will come from that."

– Melissa Etheridge

"The greatest healing therapy is friendship and love."

– Hubert H. Humphrey

Thoughtful Facebook post

You never really know where and when your life lessons are going to pop up. Sometimes they are as subtle as noticing the grace of God in the beauty of a snowflake. At other times, they arrive in a slightly less delicate form, like noticing the best-before date on the carton of milk after you've taken a mouthful. Or realizing that your fly has been down for the entirety of your presentation, thereby giving your audience weeks of inter-office laughter and bringing new meaning to the term "PowerPoint." In my experience, the universe is not only friendly, it has a wicked sense of humour.

Its timing is also flawless.

This morning I found myself sliding down one of those little slippery slopes of gloom that come from spending too much time alone with too little perspective and enjoying too little laughter. Solitude, I am afraid, is a necessary evil of the writing life, but if one is not careful to temper it with companionship, society and some form of conversation outside of the screaming voices in one's own head, one is liable to find oneself in a dark, unhappy place. And I'm not talking about Keswick.

Luckily, as I say, the universe is friendly and for some reason beyond me seems to take inordinate pleasure in repeatedly redeeming my sorry butt.

Sliding headfirst into the doldrums this morning, I chanced to open my computer to my Facebook page. There, smartly delivered by the powers that be, in a place I would be sure to take heartfelt note of it, was a post from an old high school friend. Today was the 19th anniversary of the death of his six-year-old child. Nineteen long years since losing his daughter. The post was not angry, nor spiteful, nor even terribly sad. It was a simple and beautifully honest testament to the acutely powerful love and pain that are part and parcel of being here—of living. The price of admission, as it were.

His words came as a timely and much-needed slap to my self-absorbed face. His grace, courage and hard-won wisdom comprised the perfect message, perfectly delivered to my spiritual inbox.

Sometimes we wonder why bad things happen to good people. Why six-year-old little girls are wrenched from the hearts of their parents. Why good friends are left to carry 19-year-old millstones around their weary necks. The answers to those questions can be difficult to see sometimes, almost impossible to understand if one is in the middle of such anguish. And yet, nothing happens for no good reason.

There is infinite intelligence and unconditional love behind every single thing that comes to pass in this world. I am convinced of that. And there is a beauty and orchestration that is staggering in its perfection and power. Most of us could be forgiven for seeing the death of a child as a senseless, cruel and heartbreaking tragedy. It's nothing I would ever wish on my worst enemy. But 19 years later, when that six-year-old angel's departure is still teaching life lessons to a 52-year-old man and probably countless others, I see the hand of God in that.

Subject: There Is No Place Like Home

To: Group
From: Neil Crone
Priority: High

There's no place like home, there's no place like home. You got that, right, Dorothy? When you're sick, or recovering or just plain worn out, you can't beat your own place. It's amazing how comforting just being around your own stuff is. It's like you are once again surrounded by a thousand little talismans, all beaming their healing power into you. Things that under normal circumstances might be an annoyance—the thrum of the dryer, the rhythmic swish and swash of the dishwasher, even the sound of the dog's nails click, click, clicking across the hardwood—are now comforting, perhaps even hypnotic, suggestions that all will soon be well. Even if you're thrashing about in bed, unable to sleep, there is a certain comfort in knowing that at least you are wide awake in your own bed. Even throwing up is always more tolerable in your own toilet.

During my early days back, when I was spending most of my time on the couch in the front room, the nicest sound of the day came around 3 p.m. I would hear the door to the family room open and slam closed followed hard by my children's happy, energetic voices shouting, "Hello, we're home!" At first their mother tried to shush them, to let their father sleep, but I vetoed that. Their voices and their laughter and light birdlike chatter, floating in from the kitchen were more potent healers than a thousand antibiotics.

I am the most fortunate man in the world, too, in that I have a wife who, apparently, was born to heal people. From the moment my illness was diagnosed, an engine inside my wife began to rev. A little two-stroke, built over two millennia ago, that runs like a top. This thing cranks out nurturing and kindness by the ladle-full. From dawn to dusk, I can hear my wife in the kitchen, pouring love and healing and hope into muffin tins and juice glasses and casserole dishes. Cancer cells are leaping out of my body like rats from a sinking ship. My wife is pissed at them, and they know it. Only the stupid and proud are still hanging around now, and she has something special planned for them. Who would've thought I'd ever feel bad for some sorry-assed cancer cells?

The only person at home who is somewhat indifferent to my situation is, of course, the dog. The dog who will not get up from his place in front of the woodstove when I need to shuffle past. The dog whose only concern was that I might develop Alzheimer's and forget where his leash is kept. The dog with his own baggage. He looks at me with a certain amount of disdain as I lie on the couch. I know what he is thinking. He is thinking that if it weren't for me, he would have that couch to himself, and he is thinking that if I am so sick, how come I don't have one of those funnel collars around my head so I will not lick myself. Yes, Dorothy, there is indeed no place like home.

Neil

"Always laugh when you can,
it is cheap medicine."

– George Gordon Byron

"The best way out is always through."

– Robert Frost

A life recorded in short, sharp notes

I've always been a journal keeper. I started filling up blank pages way back in my early teens when some insightful person bought me a thing called *The Nothing Book*. Remember those? Just a plain hardcover book full of blank pages begging to be scribbled in. I've since filled dozens of journals in all shapes and sizes. Some no more than cheap, spiral-bound note pads, others richly clad collections of inviting vellum.

And, although the contents over the years have never amounted to anything more than mental and emotional dreck— "brain droppings" as George Carlin would say—*The Nothing Book* really is an unfortunate misnomer. These journals are very much something books. They are vastly important to me, not so much for their content, but for their therapeutic value. Over the years writing has become so

much more than merely a satisfying vocation. It has become my sanity.

Writing things down, however haphazardly, helps me make sense of my world. The downloading of thought onto paper makes precious room in my fevered, overcrowded mind for that illusive little jewel known as perspective.

For years I hung onto my journals, the thinking being that at some point in time I would be able to hand these rare collections of hard-wrought experience down to my own troubled offspring. I had visions of myself sitting down opposite one of my emotionally muddled adolescent children, smiling knowingly as I opened one of these magical tomes to some perfect passage that would explain it all. Because I had already been there, I could help my own kids avoid some of life's traps and pitfalls. I would be Ward Cleaver, Charles Ingalls and Norman Vincent Peale all wrapped up in one beatific idiot.

This, of course, is misguided thinking. For starters, everyone has to find their own way, and my kids' way will, in all likelihood, not be my way. It will be their very own unique way with its own unique challenges and problems that only they can deal with. And secondly, all it took was a cursory glance back into some of those magical entries to realize that most of it, if not all, was pure drivel—self-absorbed, navel-gazing twaddle of no value to anyone in the present time. It was, in fact, embarrassing.

So, I burned them. In a psychotherapeutic ritual I fed them, one at a time, into the roaring flames of the woodstove and metaphorically incinerated my past. I was surprised by the tremendous release I felt. All that was missing was some chanting, the beating of drums and the drinking of some mystical potion. I settled on a couple of fingers of single malt as a perfectly satisfactory substitute.

I still journal. I still have a number of filled journals on my shelves. I don't think I'll be burning these, however. Unlike the books of my youth, these are now mostly filled with good things. Positive memories, happy observations and hope-filled dreams. To be certain, there is the odd dark passage. I'm still very much on my journey after all, but by and large I've realized that there is much more power in writing words of appreciation than desperation. Taking note of the beauty and blessings in our lives definitely puts us in the right frame of mind to receive more of the same. I didn't know that when I was young. Now that I think of it, perhaps that's really the only journal entry worth sharing with my own kids.

Subject: Tumour Humour

To: Group
From: Neil Crone
Priority: High

Hi again everybody. Thanks for reading and catching up. Sorry if it's been some time since my last tome. I've been down and out for a while. Think I may have hit rock bottom last week. Or at least a reasonable facsimile. Just after week two of the radiation and chemo combo (that's biggie-sized), the industrial-strength diarrhea arrived on the scene. Oh yeah, folks, this was freaking biblical. Nothing was staying in me for more than a few minutes. Even that anti-Christ of the church of fibre, Wonder Bread, had a "Go Straight to Exit" card. Do not pass GO, do not visit intestineland at all—take only photographs, leave only footprints.

My oncologist, who by the by is warming up a little, smiles now, and Suzanne and I think he may even have made a joke a while ago—it was hard to tell, though. He's the kind of guy who can make a knock-knock joke sound like a death sentence. Anyway, he was actually quite terrific about this turn of events, even, dare I say it, *empathetic*. He gave me a week off chemo and asked the radiation guys to do the same. But I guess the radiation guys are in a different union or just don't take guff from any oncologists because they insisted upon my continuing the treatment.

Well, that lasted until Wednesday morning when things had deteriorated to the point where Suz and I didn't think I could make the car ride down to Sunnybrook unless one of us was wearing

Depends and maybe a snorkel. After a couple of phone calls, radiation finally caved and gave me the rest of the week off. Hallelujah!

I'm now back on the chemo pump, although at a lower dosage than before, and I'm going to radiation in the evenings. I get two injections a day now, full of some wonder drug that is supposed to help the diarrhea immensely and also fight tumour growth (almost sounds as good as Crest, doesn't it?). So far, home-care nurses have been sticking me with the needles, but tonight, Suzanne, who I hope to God has been paying very close attention, is going to try her hand at it.

Actually, I am sure she will be a natural. Prior to this, she had taken over the saline flushes and Heparin injections to my PICC line, and it was like falling off a log to her. The woman can do anything. Still, if you think I'll have my eyes open during this first attempt with the needle tonight, you're dreaming.

Aside from the trots, I'm feeling OK. The nausea is manageable most of the time, especially if I can keep my mind on something else. I hardly even notice the PICC line anymore, and even the pump seems like an old friend. Well, not friend really, more like say, an old shop teacher or that old lady down the block that your mom always said you had to be polite to, even though her breath was brutal and she looked weird.

I've almost shaved my head. They told me my hair would not be affected by the chemo, but they lied. The bastards. I noticed a few weeks ago that it was getting mighty thin up top. I looked in the mirror one morning and saw Mr. Roper looking back. That was the end of that. I gave the clippers to Suz and had her do a pre-emptive strike. She took it right down to the wood. And I kind of like it. Sure is low maintenance. Good news for a guy who hasn't been able to shower for the last month. I take baths all the time now, and I lie down with my PICC arm sticking straight up in the air. I look like some businessman ordering a schnapps in the steam room.

Spiritually and emotionally I'm hanging in. Thanks, in large part, to so many of you who somehow manage to send your love along always at just the right moment. I may have mentioned this before, but I really cannot tell you how awestruck Suz and I have become as we watch the universe looking after us. I know that may sound loopy to a lot of you, but believe me, when you've witnessed enough doors opening just in the nick and arms appearing to catch you when you thought for sure this was the time you were going to hit the floor, you quickly become a believer.

Case in point: in the middle of perhaps my darkest moment of last week—when I just did not feel I could take another step in this whole journey—a letter arrived. I didn't recognize the name on the return address. I opened it and read the most beautiful note from a young woman. She was a reader of my column and felt moved to write to me, telling me of her mother's incredible battle with breast cancer. She told me about her mother dancing at her 40th wedding anniversary party with her chemo pump over her dress. She told me about her mother's laughter and her spirit, which was as bright as the sun right up until the disease claimed her this past April. It was one of the loveliest things I had ever read, and it came at the exact time I needed to hear something like that.

Suzanne came into the kitchen to find me bawling my eyes out. "What's wrong, honey?" she asked, putting her arms around me.

"Pretty…letter" was all I could gurgle out between sniffles.

That kind of thing happens all the time. There is not a week goes by where warm arms do not reach out from somewhere to encircle us both. It really is something.

Anyway, I see that I have gone on for some time already. In closing, let me say that I miss you all so much. But we're just now passing the halfway mark of all of this bullshit, and I know it will not be long before I see many of you in the flesh once again. Those of you I have not yet seen in the flesh might want to start working out.

I love every one of you with the strength of ten Grinches plus two.

Neil

"When the Japanese mend broken objects, they aggrandize the damage by filling the cracks with gold. They believe that when something's suffered damage and has a history, it becomes more beautiful."

– Barbara Bloom

"I don't think of all
the misery but of the beauty
that still remains.

– Anne Frank

A flickering flame ignites meaning

I'm travelling today. Heading off to spend some time with and say goodbye to a dying friend. I'm not sure whether it's another lesson of having come through my adventure with cancer, but I find there is something intensely clarifying about being around someone who is about to make their transition.

I don't know of anything more valuable or vital to those of us still healthy and carrying on. Everything—and I mean everything—is cast in a more brilliant hue when you are near someone whose flame is obviously flickering. I suppose it's the final gift the dying hand to us. But just behind the grief and the sadness and the loss, there is a very urgent message flashing across our consciousness. It's as though every cell in our bodies were suddenly shouting at the top of their tiny amoebic lungs, "Get going! Let's live! What the hell are you waiting for?"

When you sit with someone who is finishing their journey here, you are confronted with the undeniable. Time is short. And that message, while startling, need not be terrifying. Indeed, if anything it should be, like the tale of Ebenezer Scrooge, a blessed wake-up call. We should come away from such encounters blazing with life energy, renewed with vigour and passion for every second we are given of breath.

I bless the dying and thank God for them. It's one of the reasons I find the obituary section of the paper the only really worthwhile reading. They are the clearest and most profound signposts any of us will come across. Time is short. Live well and joyfully, take risks and love as though your very life depended upon it. It does.

My time today with my dear friend, Wendy, is doubly poignant for me. We were both diagnosed with our various cancers around the same time. For some reason I was able to leave mine behind while sweet Wendy was bound to hers for years of remission and recurrence, remission and recurrence. An exhausting journey to be sure, but one overflowing with lessons for those of us on the outside looking in. "There, but for the grace of God, go I" is a phrase I am well acquainted with, believe me—and in no small way, because of Wendy.

I sometimes wonder if occasionally people come here with only one mission in mind: to be a vivid reminder to the rest of us to get off our sorry asses and live. If indeed that is the case, then could we ever love enough these ones who leave us so early?

I hope, when I get to her, that she will still be able to hear me. For that is the message that I would like to give her. A thank-you note, of sorts. A moment of holding her hand in mine and perhaps a gentle kiss on the cheek to let her know that, for at least one sorry-assed individual, her reminder—so bravely sent and courageously held to—was received and duly noted. Mission accomplished, Wendy. Thank you for your love and grace.

Subject: The Two Goodbyes

To: Group
From: Neil Crone
Priority: High

I said goodbye to two old friends this week. One farewell was forever, the other, I greatly hope, only a temporary distancing.

The latter was my neighbour and dear friend (we'll call him Agamemnon), who is relocating to a different town two or three hours away. Not since I was a kid can I remember that sad, empty, feeling of a pal moving out of the neighbourhood. I'm feeling it again now. For even though we all say we'll stay in touch, write, email, phone etc., inevitably distance outweighs all good intention, the swift current of a busy life sweeps us along, and ties are loosened or simply allowed to dissolve. Doesn't that always seem to be the way?

But for now, I am missing my friend a great deal. And not in the way where I no longer have a twice weekly lunch buddy or squash partner or fishing pal. Aggie and I never did any of those things. In point of fact, we seldom saw each other throughout the week. But my friend was a kindred spirit—that rarest of person with whom you automatically connect and feel safe baring your throat to. The kind of friend who groks your weirdest ideas immediately and picks up on the subtlest of your sarcasm simply because you share the same wavelength. Friends like that don't need to see each other a lot. It's just nice to know they're nearby. Friends like that, as I say, are rare. Rarer still among men, who are more often than not reluctant to comfortably go beyond a slap on the back and a cold beer in the hand. And so, yes, I will miss my friend Agamemnon. We still had a lot of precious ground to cover.

My other goodbye, the one I made to a friend I hope never to see again, was of a more complex nature. After six long weeks, I finally said so long to my chemo pump. You may think that six weeks is not a particularly long time for a relationship to develop, but this was a twenty-four hour a day, seven day a week affair. We went everywhere together. We were, quite literally, inseparable. At first, I must tell you, I hated him. I found him loud, intrusive and annoying. For most of those six weeks I couldn't wait to be rid of him. I loudly and repeatedly cursed his damnable presence, and several times I came within a hair's breadth of drastic measures. But strangely, over the last few days of our tenure together, I found myself softening. The scales fell from my eyes and I realized, not quite too late I hope, that what I thought was a poisonous enemy was perhaps the best friend I may ever have had. The brute may have been bothersome and sickening, but his sole purpose, I now understand, was to save my life. And he may well have done just that.

So, here I am alone with my regrets. Regrets on the one hand for things unsaid and on the other for things said perhaps too loudly. I suppose there's a lesson in there somewhere.

Neil

"The most important thing in illness is never to lose heart."

–Nikolai Lenin

"To heal is to touch with love
that which we previously
touched with fear."

– Stephen Levine

Waste it or taste it, life always goes on

By the time you read this I will have turned 50. And the rumours, by the way, are true. Not about me and that Danish juggler, but about time. It does go by in a flash. Life is such a sneaky little bastard, isn't it? It lulls us into complacently whiling away our time until one day we wake up and it occurs to us, "Good Lord...I'm middle-aged."

And it's not the age itself that gets to you. It's the speed of it all. It's kind of like making love. I'm usually having so much fun that by the time it's over, I can't believe a whole five minutes has gone by. But when you stop for just a moment, on your 50th—or for that matter on your 40th or 60th or whatever—and you realize that five decades have gone by in the blink of an eye, that's a corker, let me tell you.

Wasn't it just yesterday I was in high school? My youth seems so richly tangible I can almost taste it. I can clearly remember riding my bike to the store to pick up some smokes for my Dad—an errand I loved because he was sure to give me the change from his bills, which I could then blow on Mojos and Ton 'O' Gum. I can still feel that kid inside me. I am still that kid.

In the larger span of life, my marriage of 24 years seems like a couple of minutes. How then did my children get to be taller than I am? How is it possible one is leaving for college? I was just burping them a second ago.

I had cancer six years ago. Even then I promised myself never to waste another moment in worry or fear or regret. To enjoy every sandwich, as Warren Zevon so brilliantly said. And I think I have. But life doesn't seem to care. It's got a schedule and it's hell-bent on keeping it.

Waste it or taste it, life always goes on. And it goes on quickly. What's even more terrifying is that it seems to be a downhill ride as well. The older we get, the faster it goes. Along with the grey hair and wrinkles we're picking up speed. This is why those first two or three decades seem to last such a good, long time. Then 40 comes along and startles the hell out of us. Suddenly we've barely got time to catch our breath when the next pitch whizzes by, 50, 60, 70—decades blowing us back like Nolan Ryan fastballs.

Still, I feel lucky. I'm very happy and I am consciously aware of why I am happy. I'm finally starting to figure it out, and it feels good. The old cliches are true. It's not how much stuff you have. It's not about where you've been or where you're going. It's not what you do. It's all about how you feel. How you feel in every single, precious moment of every fleeting day. It's not the destination, it's the ride. It's always been about the ride. I get that now. I'm also learning that the secret to a long, happy life does not seem to have nearly as much to do with exercise or nutrition or getting a flu shot as it does with two little words: thank you. Take daily and repeat as often as feels good.

Subject: Update from Cancer Command

To: Group
From: Neil Crone
Priority: High

Hi everybody,

Well, here we all are once again. I'm feeling pretty good today. The last two weeks weren't really great ones. Not nearly as much fun as the first go-round. The chemo nailed me much harder this time. I'm wondering if maybe they give you a little more each round—you know, just for a gag, to see if you notice. This time around I was plagued by mouth sores. My throat became inflamed to the point that it was difficult to swallow for a few days. And for some reason yawning was brutally painful. Needless to say I stayed away from watching the political debates or anything involving Howie Mandel. My lower lip took the brunt of the damage, though. For the last week, I've looked like some poor bastard out of the Franklin Expedition—covered in yellow, scabby sores that would tear off in my sleep, and well, you get the picture. And, oh yeah, did I mention the diarrhea? How remiss of me. The chemo eats away at any cells that replicate quickly, good and bad, so it goes after your GI tract big time. The result is that your food goes through you faster than an otter on a waterslide. With that, of course, comes the obligatory gas. And I'm not talking about toots here, folks. I'm talking about stuff that makes Passchendaele look like a cakewalk. Satellite photos are revealing a new hole in the ozone layer over Sunderland. We'll be watching television together and I'll get an attack, and before I know it Suzanne and the boys will be crawling out of the room on their bellies, Suzanne yelling, "Pee on your handkerchiefs! Pee on your handkerchiefs!" It's not pretty. But we learn to laugh at it. At least I do.

I'm realizing, slowly, that so much of this battle is mental. You can't feel the chemo going into your body and the needle only hurts briefly, but your mind, and maybe every cell in your body, is screaming, "Don't put this shit in here! What are you, nuts? This is poison! You're gonna get the shits again, pal!"

The result (at least for me) is that you get a very strong psychosomatic reaction to the whole process. I start to get nauseous the moment we walk into the hospital. The smell of rubbing alcohol can almost make me hurl. When you sit in the chair to get your drugs they give you something cold to put into your mouth to dilate the blood vessels (as I mentioned earlier the chemo goes for the mouth and the GI tract quickly) to limit the damage of the drug. You have your choice of vanilla ice cream, Popsicles or crushed ice. Over the past two sessions, I have tried them all and now cannot bear to even think about any of the three without wanting to toss my cookies. Those of you who have visited a Dairy Queen in my presence will understand how remarkable it is to picture Neil Crone with an aversion to ice cream. Geez, last summer Kawartha Dairy was inches away from releasing its new flavour, Crone Crunch. I was part of their business plan. It's remarkable; I cannot stop myself from making these negative associations. My greatest fear is that, because the drugs are administered by female nurses, I will develop a nauseous reaction to women (or at least women in a nurses uniform…which will totally ruin Thursday nights once a month in our bedroom).

So, we are slowly and sometimes painfully inching our way through this obstacle course. I go downtown to Sunnybrook tonight to see the radiation people and get my belly tattooed for their bombsites. I wonder if they can do something creative, like a hula dancer or something incorporating my navel. The radiation will begin on a nightly basis on, believe it or not, July 5, our 18th wedding anniversary. There's a terrifically dark irony in the act of irradiating the hell out of somebody's gonads on the night of his honeymoon. Again, you have to laugh.

In another week or so, I will be having a PICC line put into my arm. It's a thin (I hope really, really thin) tube that is inserted into a vein in my biceps and runs up my arm, over the shoulder and down over the heart. The end sticking out of the arm is attached to a tube, which in turn is attached to a small battery-powered pump that I will carry around in a fanny pack for five weeks. It's a continuous infusion of chemo during that period. I only report to the hospital once a week for refills. I wonder if they give coupons.

I'd be lying if I said that a lot of this stuff doesn't frighten me. It does. I'm not looking forward at all to having a tube snaked into me like some Roto-Rooter. And I'm wondering like hell what five weeks of this junk inside me will do to me. But, I am doing my best, and with the help of my wonderful, amazing, patient, loving and very curvy wife (my sex drive will be the last thing the chemo touches, folks, if I have to shunt every last platelet in my body down there), I am learning to dwell very much in the present. One day at a time and don't look too far ahead. Worrying avails us nothing. Every day is a mental discipline. Today is the first day of the rest of your life, blah, blah, blah…

You know what really gets me through? The end. I think about the end. I think about the cool, colourful days of the fall and my boys' birthdays and the last time I walk out of that damned hospital. I'm gonna French kiss a nurse and maybe even my oncologist on that day. I'm gonna drop my pants and moon my chemo chair. And then I am going to take my family on a trip to somewhere warm and sandy where the only thing cold that goes in my mouth comes from a brewery. I think about that, folks. I think about that a lot.

Once again, my heartfelt thanks to all of you for your love and support. You have to be in my shoes to really know how much it all means, but believe me every one of your emails and notes is a lifesaver. I can't tell you on how many occasions a very dark moment has been relieved by a word or two of caring. Keep those cards and letters coming, folks.

Heaps of love to you all,

Neil

"Confidence and hope do more good than physic."

– Galen

"Our illness
is often our healing."

– Mooji

Hit rock bottom—things are looking up

I'm not sure if this falls firmly into the too-much-information category, but this week marks the last of my annual colonoscopies. From here on in, my surgeon tells me, I can go on the normal routine of once every five years. Just like a regular person.

Gosh, what will I do with myself? I wonder if I'll go through any kind of colono-scopic withdrawal. Only an actor would miss getting a yearly colonoscopy—anytime near a camera is a good time, right? And the "biz" has been a little slow lately.

I certainly won't miss the prep day. For those of you who have never undergone a colonoscopy, the actual "scoping" procedure, although it sounds medieval, is really a cakewalk. It's like college frosh week—you're unconscious for most of it. The prep day, however, is a different animal al-together. Have you ever watched what happens when your kids dump a pack of Mentos into a litre bottle of Coke? The two little packets of prep powder produce an equally explosive response, only inside you. And you can't screw the cap on this one.

My first time through this drill, I found out the hard way they really mean it when they say, "You must be close to a washroom while taking the bowel prep." In point of fact, they should be even more specific: "You must be clearly in sight of an unoccupied washroom while taking the bowel prep." An equally helpful admonishment might be "Are you certain you want to do this?"

This stuff is like having a volcano in your pants. And like the residents of Pompeii, you don't get a whole lot of lead time. The rest of your family, therefore, needs to be hip to it as well. There's nothing like having your colon go all Vesuvius on you while your teenager is in the bathroom, blithely gelling his hair and trowelling on the Axe. No, when Dad is running in rocket-trouser mode, the bathrooms and all their approach lanes need to be as vacant as the Air Canada Centre in the playoffs.

And this goes on for a full day. Fortunately, as a self-unemployed artist, it's not a big deal for me to stay at home and ride it out. What's truly terrifying, though, is that some people probably try to do this while on the job.

"Good morning, folks, this is your captain speaking. Welcome aboard Flight 992 to Calgary. We're currently cruising at 22,000 feet with an air speed of… whoopsie…back in a flash."

The actual colonoscopy, as I have mentioned, is really a non-event. They put you under, you wake up, you fart, you go home. I've been on dates that were more troublesome. I remember vividly, at my first scope, years ago, walking into the endoscopy suite and seeing this thick, black tubular thing coiled on a hook on the wall. I half-jokingly said to my surgeon, "That's the case, right? It's actually a lot smaller than that?" No.

That was, in fact, the camera. But anesthesia is a wonderful thing. So is modern health care. I'm walking, talking, writing proof of that.

And one thing that is often overlooked in all this talk about prep and scopes and anaconda-sized cameras is that someone has the unenviable yet life-savingly important task of peeking up our backsides to make sure we're good to go. Our doctors and nurses.

And those wonderful people I will miss.

Subject: Diarrhea, Diarrhea!

To: Group
From: Neil Crone
Priority: High

Dear friends,

Hello again. Criminy, I can't believe it's been almost a month since I last wrote to everyone. Time flies when you're killing off malignant cells. I'm sorry about not keeping up. Don't know where the time has gone. God knows I haven't really been busy or anything. I'm into the first week off of a three-week hiatus from chemo. I must say that last week's round in the chair actually seemed so much better than what I had been going through. Everything is relative, I suppose. I even drove myself to my treatments this time around. Suz would've come—in fact, I think it was driving her nuts that she couldn't be there with me—but both boys had come down with something during that first week of school and she needed to be here with them. My appointments were at the ungodly hour of 7:15 in the morning— every day too. Which meant getting up at 5:30 a.m. The nice thing about that, though, was there was never any lineup at the salad bar at that time of day. Nothing worse than trying to elbow some bald, 80-year-old woman away from the coleslaw when you're not feeling great. "Yeah, I know you got cancer, sweetheart—we all do! Now back in line, sugar!"

Anyway, driving myself actually seemed to help a bit. Focusing on driving made it much easier not to focus on throwing up. A good trade-off. I ended up having a pretty uneventful week. Only really felt awful when I was actually getting the injections. And that, more than anything, is still a mental thing. It's frightening how strong that negative association is—even sitting here writing about it makes my gorge rise. If you want to know what I'm talking about try thinking about *The Mike Bullard Show* for a few minutes. See what I mean?

This week I feel pretty well. And a large part of that is that I can finally see light at the end of this damn tunnel. I have one more week of chemo (and it's only a four-day week courtesy of Thanksgiving Monday; bless you, Pilgrims), and hopefully it will be the last one in my lifetime. I'm feeling kind of like a kid when he's only got that last piece of broccoli on his plate, and he knows if he can just choke that sucker down then there's a big wedge of apple pie waiting with his name on it. I'm still struggling with fatigue and a few mouth sores. And of course, I've dealt with it for so long that it just feels normal to have diarrhea most of the time. (If I go to the john less than six times a day, I feel constipated.) But all that is much easier to deal with just knowing that it will soon be over and the real healing can begin. My friend Ray emailed me the other day (Ray is my hero who has been through all of this and worse), and he mentioned in his letter what a strange thing it is to be in recovery for so long that you begin to forget what good health actually feels like. It's true. I've lost touch with that feeling of waking up and feeling whole. Mostly I just wake up because of my hole. But it's coming back slowly.

My morning walk continues to be the highlight of my day. Ianto (dog with issues) and I head out just after we get the boys off to school, around 8:30, and we're usually gone for a little over a half an hour. I could walk through the country for hours if I had the strength. I can't tell you what peace those early morning hours bring. I'm actually starting to freak a little about going back to normal life. In a way I've been badly spoiled these last six months. I've driven into Toronto a couple of times to record some overdue voice stuff, and each time the drive nearly killed me. When you've suddenly had the extended warranty on your life removed, four precious hours of it lost to gridlock each day seems unforgivable. I may have to rethink this commuting thing.

I don't miss the "biz" at all, really. And frankly, that's come as a bit of a surprise to me. I miss the people, my friends and their wonderful senses of humour, I miss kibitzing at auditions, but I'd be lying if I said I couldn't wait to get back to spending 14-hour days in a 4 x 8 cubicle waiting to play Cop #4, or sitting in a casting office with 50 other people, waiting to see which of us can say, "Honey, my shirt smells great!" the best. Call me kooky, but at some point that lost its gloss. I guess this thing has affected me in more ways than I had thought. Friends who have gone through it told me it would. I just thought, at the time, that they were a bunch of cancer survivor liars, I guess.

But I am happy, folks. The things that are the purest and the truest and the strongest have not changed one iota for me during all of this. I still have the best partner in the world in the unsinkable Suzanne, my children are godsends every day, and my family and friends never cease to amaze me with their love and support. I have a lot of giving back to do. A job, unlike Cop #4, I greatly look forward to.

Loads of love to you all. I hope this finds each and every one of you glowing with health and happiness,

Neil

"Cancer is enough
to get my attention."

– Charles Grodin

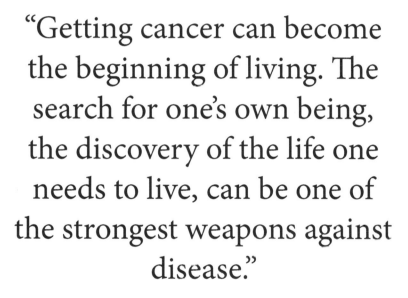

"Getting cancer can become the beginning of living. The search for one's own being, the discovery of the life one needs to live, can be one of the strongest weapons against disease."

– Lawrence Leshan

Health care big and small reveals insights

Some people like to spend a long weekend at the cottage. Others enjoy a family road trip. Still others like to simply stay at home and putter around the garden. Whenever I get two or three days off in a row, I like to hang out at hospital emergency wards. At least that's the way it seemed this past weekend.

Through a series of gastrointestinal (mine) and cardiopulmonary (my father's) irregularities, I spent Friday through Saturday evening—and the better part of Monday—in two separate hospitals. Because of some form of divine intervention, I managed to avoid the health-care system on the Sabbath.

Although my colon still tends to operate with the reliability of a Sea King helicopter, I am once again home and happy, and Dad is, while still hospitalized, resting comfortably and on the mend. But aside from the differences in our particular maladies, what struck me over the head like a Taylor reflex hammer was the difference in our levels of care.

Because Dad's condition was slightly more critical than mine (I couldn't fart, he couldn't breathe), he was ambulanced to the nearest facility capable of dealing with his complex medical needs—a large urban hospital.

The doctors and nurses there are all highly trained, dedicated individuals. I saw first-hand the kind of talent these people possess, as they quickly attended to my father.

But it is also a very busy, very stressed, city hospital. The ER waiting room looked like a mosh pit. Swarms of people looking for medical attention filled every chair, gurney and vacant corner, with more flowing through the doors all the time.

Canadians are lucky as hell to have a health-care system that looks after us the way it does. But make no mistake, there are times when that system is strained to the breaking point. Patients here were stacked up like cordwood, waiting for a bed, and it was many hours before Dad was lucky enough to be admitted into a semi-private room.

Conversely, my wife drove me to Port Perry Hospital just after midnight, early Saturday, and it was like pulling into Petticoat Junction. Triage was so empty we could've square-danced.

In a moment, Hank the security guard sleepily sauntered out from his bunk—and in a kindly manner directed us to the admitting station. In less time than it took for Dad to get his blood pressure back to normal, I was hooked up to an IV and happily shaking hands with my old pal, Dr. Morphine.

I spent the night in emergency but, even with the comings and goings of a number of patients, it was a relatively peaceful night. It was Walden Pond compared to Dad's ordeal.

I don't mean to intimate rural hospitals don't get busy. They are, after all, at the epicentre of two of the most dangerous activities in the world, farming and cottaging. Think I'm joking? Ask any ER nurse up here how many fish hooks she's taken out of people. And have you been near any farm equipment lately?

Still, I received extraordinary treatment. So friendly and fresh-scrubbed were my various nurses, I began to think I was in the middle of an Ivory Soap casting session. And the doctors and technicians were incomparable. I passed my second night there in a private room with a view onto a lovely treed courtyard. Dad's window doesn't open.

Say what you will about small towns, I'm really glad I live where I live.

Subject: Last Chapter

To: Group
From: Neil Crone
Priority: High

Dear friends,

This will be, I sincerely hope, the last correspondence I make to you from Cancer Central. I do believe we are finally at the end. Well, the end of the chemo and radiation anyway. What a strange and wonderful journey this has been. I find myself caught in a sense of weird timelessness. Most of the usual markers are gone from me, the things I used to gauge the passage of my life with—work, schedule, deadlines, even daily chores. I seem to have been floating through these last six months, waiting, hoping to get to this point, the end.

So, some realignment is due, I suppose. That will be good. I feel ready for work now, eager to get back into life at more of a contributor level. As my health and energy return, I find myself looking forward to the challenge of my work once again—auditions, studying, performance. I want to take the load from Suzanne, who has carried so much for so long. I want to give her a rest, to let her focus on her life for a while.

These last two chemo rounds have been very tolerable. A half an hour in the chair every morning for a week and then three weeks off to recoup. I have found them much easier than the middle of the summer with the pump and the nightly drill of radiation. Perspective is everything. Last Friday, my last day in the oncology ward, was a strange one. I was immensely happy to be leaving. I brought the nurses a bouquet of flowers as an inadequate thank you, and when the time came to get up out of the chair for the last time I actually felt very sad—mostly because of those still in the chairs. They cheered me and waved with intravenoused arms, but their eyes, bless them, looked so tired. There was an older woman seated next to me on that last day. We'd been chair neighbours for the week, and as such I couldn't help but overhear some of her conversations with her husband and son, who accompanied her each day. She had been 185 pounds when she started her treatments and had had lush shoulder-length hair. She was now 109 pounds and had the scalp of an ostrich. She came to her chair every morning in a wheelchair, wrapped in blankets to keep out the chill that seemed to be always with her. She was in the chair long after I left each day. And yet, she still found the strength to laugh on occasion and always had a smile for the nurses. I found her quite amazing, and on my last day of chemo I told her so. I reached over to touch her shaking hands, and I told her what an inspiration she was to me. I thanked her for putting my own complaints in their proper place. She smiled a beautiful smile and whispered that she was glad of that. I could have picked her up and carried her home at that point.

And so, yes, my heart broke a little bit as I blew a kiss to the room and wished them all good health. I hope they're all out of there soon. As for me, I couldn't get out of that damned hospital fast enough. That night, Suzanne and I held a champagne toast and chemo-card-burning celebration for a few neighbours and family. I wish we could have had all of you there. But there is still time for that, my friends, still time for that.

I didn't know how much strength I'd have for celebrating that night, but we simply couldn't let this hallmark pass without some kind of *fête*. So, after some toasts and thank yous, we placed my chemo cards on a specially selected silver platter and burned the fuckers. It felt pretty good. It felt even better to have a house filled with laughter and the warm voices of friends. I hadn't laughed that much in a while. It was particularly nice to see Suzanne letting go and playing again. I could see the weight falling off of her lovely shoulders.

So, here we are. This week is passing well. The side effects from last week's dosage have been very manageable, although poor Suzanne has had to make her morning coffee out in the garage, as the smell (for some weird reason) suddenly makes me want to retch. But that will pass in a few days. Three nights a week she and I and Connor are in rehearsals for *The Nerd*—a play we are doing with a local group in Uxbridge. It's been a much-needed diversion from nausea and a great source of laughter for all of us. A good stepping stone back into performance too.

And, very soon, I hope to be seeing you all again. If my energy levels continue to climb as they have, I don't see why I couldn't be back backstabbing other actors in a week or so.

I guess, then, it's time to close the book on this thing. It's remarkable how bittersweet I find writing this to be. You have all helped so much in the passage of this illness that I am a little reluctant to let go. Perhaps I should end by taking a page out of my own chemo book and telling you that you have all been a huge inspiration to me and more. Let me leave you by blowing all of you a kiss as well and wishing you everlasting health.

Yours in the greatest of love and affection,

Neil

"A good laugh and a long sleep are the best cures in the doctor's book."

– Irish Proverb

"Disease is somatic;
the suffering from it, psychic."

– Martin H. Fischer

Trick colons and men in skirts don't mix

The universe, I am convinced, has a wicked sense of humour. Recently I was invited to host a charity fundraiser. The theme of the evening was "Bombay Nights" and so I thought, as the host, it might be fun to dress the part. I did a little shopping and got myself a smart maroon kurta and off-white pants. The kurta is like a long shirt that hangs down to about the knees and when worn with the baggy, tapering trousers, creates a very handsome, very comfortable, very Indian look. Perfect. Not only did I look and feel elegant in theme, but I wasn't going to have to wear a tie. Always a plus in my book.

The only downside to the event was that Bombay Nights happened to be taking place on a February night. And this particular February night was laden with some weather that was not terribly "kurta friendly." There

wasn't enough curry in the world to keep me from freezing my bindi off in that outfit.

So I had to bundle up as best I could. I cut quite a figure in my winter coat with the maroon dress billowing out from beneath and my off-white legs shoved into enormous galoshes. I looked like a bag lady in a pair of queen-sized pantyhose. Still, no biggie. Barring any unforeseen difficulties, I'd be privately ensconced in my car for the drive down and then quickly inside the hall where I could whisk off the cold-weather paraphernalia and reveal my true Bollywood splendour.

Now, at this point in the narrative, I should mention that, since having a portion of my plumbing removed, along with a tumour, a number of years ago, my pipes have been somewhat finicky. I'm ecstatic to still be alive, but my gastrointestinal tract now runs with the reliability of a Skoda. These colonic hiccups are not really an issue as long as I am in the comfort and safety of my own home. I've also learned, over the years, that if I do have to venture out, and in particular if I'm to be in the public eye, forewarned is definitely forearmed. For hours prior to a gig I don't generally ingest anything more volatile than a soda cracker. It's just safer that way.

On this day, however, I threw caution to the wind and ate an oatmeal cookie. An oatmeal cookie laced with castor oil, apparently.

Fifteen minutes down the road, just diabolically far enough en-route to make turning back an impossibility, bowel Armageddon struck.

Like the *Hindenburg* or the wreck of the *Edmund Fitzgerald*, these things are always funny in retrospect, but at the time, not so much. I was desperate. So desperate that I frantically wheeled into the parking lot of a public school, left my wife with the motor running and tore, cheeks clenched, into the building.

I can only imagine, in a post-9/11 world, what might go through the head of any staff member witnessing a crazed man in a kurta dashing, wild-eyed, into the nearest john. I'm sure the scenario would end badly. Miraculously, however, the only person I encountered was a lone school bus driver who was leaning against her vehicle, chatting on a cellphone as I exited the building some blessed minutes later. Her conversation came to an abrupt halt as she caught sight of me, her slitted eyes tracking me across the parking lot, fingers blindly groping for the digits 9-1-1.

As I say, it's funny now. But I don't think I ever want to know just how close I came to eating soda crackers in my cell at Guantanamo.

"We are survivors from the moment of diagnosis."

– Peter Jennings

"Today is the first day of my second life."

– Seiji Ozawa

About the Author

Neil Crone has been a fixture in Canadian television for years, starring in such shows as *Wind at My Back* and CBC's award-winning *Little Mosque on the Prairie*. Besides acting and public speaking, Neil is a prolific writer. In addition to his weekly column in select Metroland newspapers entitled "Enter Laughing," a collection of his early columns have been published in an anthology entitled *Enter Laughing: The Early Years.*

Neil has also written two children's books. The first, *Who Farted? Stories in Verse for Big & Little Kids,* is a fun and whimsical collection of children's poetry. The second, *The Farmers' Secret Midnight Dance,* is a beautiful story of magic and discovery. Both books are illustrated by Canadian cartoonist Wes Tyrell.

Neil's books are published by Wintertickle Press and are available online and in fine book-selling establishments—independent and otherwise.

To learn more about Neil Crone, please feel free to check out his website at **www.neilcrone.com**.

Connect

Facebook: **semicolonbook**
winterticklepress
Twitter: **@wintertickle**